Journeying

through Lent

with Luke

JOURNEYING
THROUGH LENT
with LUKE

DAILY MEDITATIONS

NANCY KOESTER

Augsburg
MINNEAPOLIS

JOURNEYING THROUGH LENT WITH LUKE
Daily Meditations

Cover photography copyright © 2000 PhotoDisc. Used by permission.
Cover design by Timothy W. Larson
Interior design by Timothy W. Larson

Library of Congress Cataloging-in-Publication Data

Koester, Nancy, –
   Journeying through Lent with Luke: daily meditations / Nancy Koester.
      p.cm.
   Includes bibliographical references (p. 122).
   ISBN 0-8066-4065-0 (alk. paper)
   1. Bible. N.T. Luke—Meditations. 2. Lent—Meditations. 3. Devotional calendars. I. Title.

BS2595.4.K64 2000
242'.34—dc21   00-049342

The paper used in this publication meets the minimum requirements of American National Standard for Information Sciences—Permanence of Paper for Printed Library Materials, ANSI Z329.48-1984.

Manufactured in the U.S.A.   AF 9-4065

05   04   03   02   01   2   3   4   5   6   7   8   9   10

CONTENTS

Week 1: Praying

Throughout the Gospel story, Jesus prayed. He taught his disciples to pray and he told stories about prayer. He often sought God in prayer and faced some of his worst temptations in prayer. Jesus' whole life was a prayer for God's kingdom to come and God's will to be done. A journey through Lent with Luke therefore begins with prayer, a theme that will be encountered again during Holy Week.

Ash Wednesday

Read Luke 18:1-8. *Pray always and do not lose heart* (v. 1).

Some people just never give up. The Russian Revolution, looters, dynamite, and decades of neglect would discourage most people. But Prince Meschersky persists in claiming his old ancestral estate in Alabino, Russia. According to the *New York Times* News Service, the Prince won't quit, although he's up against eighty-plus years of brutal history. Meschersky, an engineer, lives with his family in an old gatehouse on the ancestral estate. The gatehouse has no heat, electricity, or running water. Location is everything: this is as close as the Mescherskys can get to the family palace. Built in 1775, this palace once housed a splendid art collection—which, along with anything else of value, was looted long ago. After the Revolution of 1917, the Meschersky family was forced to leave. In the 1930s the palace became a holding camp for prisoners arrested by Stalin's secret police. Finally the palace was blown up by the Communists who wanted the rubble for road building. Nothing remains of the once elegant home but a hollow shell. "The Prince" has been a squatter here for several years now, attempting to reclaim the ancestral estate. Under the post-Communist Russian constitution, Meschersky claims the right to inherit and to hold property. As of the year 2000, authorities had not agreed to the engineer's claims, but neither had they evicted Meschersky.

The Prince's story models persistence, a key to prayer. Jesus teaches people to pray and never give up. In Luke 18:2-8 he tells of a widow who has been wronged by someone. Perhaps she has been evicted from her home or deprived of her income; Jesus does not say. But to obtain justice for her cause, the widow pesters a judge until he finally settles the case in her favor. This judge cares nothing for justice or compassion. "I have no fear of God and no respect for anyone," he declares, "yet because this widow keeps bothering me, I will grant her justice, so that she may not wear me out by continually coming" (Luke 18:4-5). Finally the widow wins her case. The judge is relieved of a nuisance and justice prevails.

This story, in which a flinty judge finally acts if only to get rid of a pest, hardly sounds like a plan for pious prayer. Yet Jesus tells the story "so that you will pray and not lose heart." After telling the story of the widow and the judge, Jesus asks, "Will not God grant justice to his chosen ones who cry to him day and night?" If a hard-hearted judge responds to a persistent widow, how much more will a loving God answer faithful prayers? To persist in prayer is to exercise faith—faith that God's justice and mercy will prevail. Earlier in the Gospel Jesus says, "Is there anyone among you who, if your child asks for a fish, will give a snake . . . or if the child asks for an egg, will give a scorpion? If you, then, who are evil know how to give good gifts to your children, how much more will the heavenly Father give the Holy Spirit to those who ask him" (Luke 11:10-13). Jesus tells his followers to exercise faith in the mercy and justice of God—even when bad things happen.

God's people are sometimes tempted to become bitter and cynical. Those who feel as though God has kept them "on hold" for too long may want to hang up on God. For such times, Jesus gives this encouragement: persist in prayer. Do not lose heart. "Will not God grant justice to his chosen ones who cry to him day and night? Will he delay in helping them? I tell you," Jesus promises, "he will quickly grant justice."

Many people cry out for mercy and justice, hoping to find these in God. So also, God wants to find that people have faith. We want God to help us, and God wants us to believe in him. So Jesus ends the parable of the widow with this question: "When the Son of Man comes, will he find faith on earth?"

QUESTIONS AND PRAYER

1. What person, problem, or issue calls you to persistent prayer?

2. To persist in prayer is to exercise faith that God's justice and mercy will prevail. How does persistent prayer change those who engage in it?

Prayer: Lord Jesus, you promised that the heavenly Father gives the Holy Spirit to those who ask him (Luke 11:13). May your people persist in prayer and trust you for the outcome. Amen.

Thursday

Read Luke 18:10-14. *"God, I thank you that I am not like other people . . ." (v. 11).*

IF ONLY PRAYERS COULD BE EDITED before they are sent. That way, false pride and contempt for others could be deleted and God would receive only a pure, polished prayer. This would cut down greatly on God's "junk mail"—all those prayers that are really just self-advertising with no interest in God or neighbor. But God gets every message and sees people as they really are, with no editing, no makeup. "Junk mail" prayers can reveal a lot about the senders, but God is moved more by one cry from the heart than by a million unsolicited advertisements. Jesus told a story about God's in-box. If the story weren't so serious, it could almost be a joke. Perhaps it is just that—a serious joke.

In Luke 18:9-14, Jesus tells the story of two men who go to the temple to pray. The first man is devout, clean living, and respected in the community. What's more, he is a Pharisee—a "church junkie," a religious professional. Of all people, this man should know how to pray! The second man is a tax collector, hated by the people for helping the Romans exact taxes from them. Tax collectors were like vultures, picking on the carcass of a subject people. This despised tax collector hardly dares to enter the temple, much less talk to God, so he hovers near the doorway, hoping that no one will recognize him. In a prayer contest between the Pharisee and the tax collector, the Pharisee has every advantage. He knows the rules and keeps them.

The Pharisee's prayer starts off on the right note: "God, I thank you. . ." (Luke 18:11). So far, so good. But immediately the Pharisee begins to preen: "'God, I thank you that I am not like other people' (Luke 18:11). I am not a thief, rogue, or adulterer. I'm not a tax collector like that man over there. I fast twice a week and give a tenth of all my income to the temple." The Pharisee is not really praying—he's just admiring his own reflection, which is surely better than anyone else's.

"Pharisee prayers" are constantly arriving in God's in-box. A classic Pharisee prayer goes like this: "I thank you, God, that I live a clean life, unlike old so-and-so." But there are infinite variations on such self-pride: "I thank you, God, that I have purged all male pronouns from everything I say, especially from worship. I thank you, God, that I am free of legalism." The joke is, of course, on all who find themselves thinking, "I thank you, God, that I am not a Pharisee."

As the Pharisee parades his accomplishments before God, the tax collector lingers at the temple door. He does not dare to come any closer or even to look up to heaven. The tax collector does not compare himself with others. He does not remind God of good deeds done. He makes no pretense, calls in no favors. In a gesture of remorse, he beats his breast and cries, "God, be merciful to me, a sinner!" (Luke 18:13).

Here's the punch line: Jesus says that it is the tax collector who goes home "justified," right with God, not the Pharisee. For "all who exalt themselves will be humbled, and all who humble themselves will be exalted" (18:14).

Jesus told this story to deflate proud people and lift up humble people. Like a needle in a medicine kit, the story both wounds and heals. It punctures and deflates false pride, but for those whose hearts are torn, it mends with the promise that God hears a plea from the heart.

Questions and Prayer

1. Why do you suppose there are so many "Pharisee prayers" in God's in-box?

2. Does the story of the Pharisee and the tax collector convict you or encourage you?

Prayer: Lord Jesus, you said that those who exalt themselves will be humbled and those who humble themselves will be exalted. You humbled yourself on the cross and were exalted in resurrection. We thank and praise you for your cross, which makes us right with God. Amen.

Friday

Read Luke 11:1-4. *"Lord, teach us to pray . . ."* (v. 1).

To learn to play the piano, a student needs a teacher who can play the piano, not a great musician. A great musician expects applause, but a great teacher encourages the beginner. A great teacher delights in helping a student make music. Of course, there are some great musicians who are also great teachers.

When it comes to prayer, Jesus is both a great prayer and teacher. The best, in fact. Jesus knows each person completely and at the same time intimately knows God's own heart and will. As Jesus helped his first disciples, he continually helps his disciples today to move beyond limited notions about prayer to truly praying: listening to and talking with God.

One day when Jesus had finished praying, one of his disciples said to him, "Lord, teach us to pray, as John taught his disciples"

(11:1). At that point, Jesus could have lectured *about* prayer—about having the proper attitude, using the right formulas, getting professional training, having the correct posture and voice tone—but instead Jesus gave the disciples a prayer.

Imagine giving a set of car keys to a teenager and saying, "Take off." It seems too simple. Does Jesus want us, like the disciples, to just start praying? Yes, that is exactly what Jesus wants. Luke 11:2-4 shows us how (see also Matt. 6:9-13):

> *Father, hallowed be your*
> *name.*
> *Your kingdom come.*
> *Give us each day our daily*
> *bread.*
> *And forgive us our sins,*
> *for we ourselves forgive*
> *everyone indebted to us.*
> *And do not bring us to the*
> *time of trial.*

Enriching as it is to think and talk and read *about* prayer, it is better still to pray. Anyone who wonders what to say can simply use Jesus' own words.

In the Lord's Prayer, as Martin Luther once said, Christians speak with God in complete confidence, as children speak to a loving father *(The Small Catechism)*. Jesus promises that God hears and answers prayer: "For everyone who asks receives, and everyone who searches finds, and for everyone who knocks, the door will be opened" (Luke 11:10). The prayer that Jesus gave can be prayed by small children, by beginners in Christianity, and by great saints. The important thing is to *pray* it, to *use* it, to *live* it.

This prayer of Jesus does not contain the words *I*, *me*, or *mine*. The prayer is for those who pray it and at the same time for others, indeed, for the whole world. All intercessory prayer—that is, prayer that asks God to help others—flows from the simple request: "Give *us* this day *our* daily bread."

The Lord's Prayer is risky, because it asks those of us who pray it to forgive as we ourselves receive forgiveness: "And forgive us our sins, for we ourselves forgive everyone who is indebted to us." People who want to remain unchanged should avoid this prayer, for we who receive grace—God's undeserved love and favor—are bound to extend that grace to others. Forgiving and being forgiven changes us.

Jesus taught people to pray, "Deliver us from evil." This is not a soft, nice prayer, because to pray it is to admit that there is evil in the world—around and within—and that only God's strong hand can help. Christians pray for God's saving help, both for our own problems and for people in need throughout the world. Like prayers for daily bread and forgiveness, "deliver us from evil" includes everyone, not just the person or persons praying. And those of us who call upon God to deliver us from evil may in turn be used by God to protect and defend others. No one can truly pray this prayer and remain the same.

Jesus did not just teach *about* prayer; he taught people to pray. He did not merely perform a prayer, he taught his disciples to "play the music." He gave them the keys, and he continues to give the keys to Christians everywhere.

Questions and Prayer

1. Which petition (request) in the Lord's Prayer is most urgent for you today? (See prayer below.)

2. If someone told you, "I want to pray, but I don't know what to say," how would you respond?

Prayer: Our Father, who art in heaven, hallowed be thy name. Thy kingdom come, thy will be done, on earth as it is in heaven. Give us this day our daily bread, and forgive us our trespasses as we forgive those who trespass against us. And lead us not into temptation, but deliver us from evil. For thine is the kingdom, and the power, and the glory, forever and ever. Amen.

Saturday

Read Luke 4:1-8. *The devil said to him, "If you are the Son of God, Command this stone to become a loaf of bread"* (v. 3).

Long before they appear at the Olympics, athletes spend years in training. Without these years of rigorous discipline, an athlete would never have his or her moment of Olympic glory. So it was for Jesus. His public ministry was built on the hidden foundation of loving obedience to God. The Gospels say that Jesus frequently went away by himself to pray. Sometimes temptations intruded, attacking Jesus at the very times he sought to be alone with God. Like an athlete who struggles against adversaries and rises above injury, Jesus was tempted in the wilderness. That great, unseen contest with Satan helped prepare Jesus for the cross. Had Jesus not been tempted by Satan, he would not know what ordinary people go through, even when they pray, nor would he win so great a victory in the end.

Jesus was "led by the Holy Spirit" in the wilderness (Luke 4:1). To be led by the Spirit is to be in prayer, walking in obedience to God. Prayer expressed Jesus' intimacy with God, the loving obedience of the Son to the Father. No wonder, then, that Satan assaulted Jesus at this particular time: If Satan could twist Jesus' prayers away from God, he could keep Jesus from doing God's will. In winning that battle, he could win the war. Satan tempted Jesus to pray for and trust in the wrong things. If Satan could not stop Jesus from praying, he could at least try to redirect Jesus' prayers away from God. But Jesus successfully resisted each new temptation. No matter what spin Satan tried to put on things, Jesus always landed on firm ground, obedient to God.

As fans of Olympic figure skating know, no matter how complex the jump or spin, the judges' final score reflects how well or how poorly the skater lands. So it is with temptation: Everyone is tempted. Even Jesus was tempted. What matters most is making a good landing, firmly within God's gracious will. Prayer can help people keep their balance amid the sudden turns of temptation when everything seems to be up in the air. Just as Jesus taught his disciples how to pray, so he set an example for facing temptation and landing well.

When Jesus had been without food for forty days and was famished with hunger, Satan said, "If you are the Son of God, turn this stone into bread" (4:3). It doesn't sound so bad—a little fast food out in the desert. After all, later on in his ministry, Jesus would feed an entire crowd with only a few loaves and fish; so why shouldn't he help himself while alone in the desert? No one would ever know. But Jesus knew that Satan was tempting him to unbelief—tempting him to say, "I don't believe that God is taking care of me, so I'll just help myself."

Such temptation comes often. When people are in need, Satan tempts, "God doesn't seem to be looking out for you. So why not just help yourself?" In such moments Satan can also appeal to pride, as he did when he said to Jesus, "If you are the Son of God, turn this stone into bread." The tempter says, "Why should an important person like you have to suffer? Surely you can take matters into your own hands! If faith in God doesn't seem to be working, why not believe in yourself? After all, God helps those who help themselves. Praying is a waste of time. Just reach out and grab whatever you need."

Jesus heard the tempter, but Jesus' answer rang out clear and strong: "We do not live by bread alone, but by every word that comes from the mouth of God" (Matt. 4:4). Jesus was hungry, but he stayed alert to the Spirit. Prayer had made him so familiar with God's voice that he knew this tempting voice now speaking to him was not the voice of God.

It has been said that desire, even hunger, can point to God as our true provider. As long as his hunger pointed to God, the true source of life, Jesus could resist temptation and remain faithful to God. Naturally when something important is lacking—be it food, love, work, or hope—this shortage can become a source of temptation. For example, a person who wants but does not have a loving spouse may be tempted to fill some needs through sex outside of marriage. Likewise, someone in debt may be attracted to gambling as a fast way to make money. Through prayer, however, the Holy Spirit can use even a painful emptiness to point us to God. Prayer helps us to remain faithful and wait for God to provide.

Questions and Prayer

1. Why was Jesus tempted during prayer?
2. How can a Christian respond to temptation during prayer?

Prayer: Gracious God, everyone is at times tempted to trust someone or something other than you. When we are so tempted, help us to walk in your gracious will. Thank you for providing all that we need. Keep us alert to your spirit and awake to your word. Amen.

First Sunday in Lent

Read Luke 4:5-13. *Satan said to Jesus, "If you, then, will worship me, it all will be yours"* (v. 7).

WHEN JESUS WAS IN THE WILDERNESS, the devil took him up to a high place and showed him in an instant all the kingdoms of the world. As this grand mirage shimmered in the desert heat, Satan says, "All this is mine and the authority has been given to me to turn it all over to you—if only you will worship me" (4:6, 7). The urge to grab for power is common enough, but this temptation is even more dangerous. Jesus is being tempted to believe that evil is in control. Claiming to be in charge, Satan boasts, "All authority has been given to me."

To anyone who believes it, this lie brings despair. If Satan really is in charge, it only makes sense to sign up with the winning team. From there, it's just a short step to great evil. "Make the lie big enough and people will believe it," as Adolf Hitler's minister of propaganda is reported to have said. This is Satan's "big lie": Evil is in control, God is not. And his big lie is evident in his tempting of Jesus, as if to say, "The world belongs to me, and if you worship me, it will all be yours." And Jesus answered firmly, "Worship the Lord your God and serve only him" (4:8).

First Satan tempted Jesus to unbelief: "God is not taking care of you, so take care of yourself and turn these stones into bread." Jesus refused. Next Satan tempted Jesus to despair: "Satan is in charge, not God, so play for the winning team." Jesus did not fall for this either, so Satan tried one last temptation. If Jesus would not surrender his faith, he might possibly be made to misuse it. Perhaps Jesus would agree to test God. With this goal in mind, Satan takes Jesus to the pinnacle of the temple and says, "If you are the Son of God, throw yourself down from here, for God will command his angels to protect you" (4:9, 10). If Jesus jumped from the heights, surely God would rescue him and everyone would recognize Jesus as God's son.

It sounds outlandish, but this temptation is common. Sometimes people of faith are tempted to think, "If I do such and so, then God must respond in a certain way," as though one could write a script and expect God to play an assigned role. When Christians fall for this temptation, prayer becomes an exercise in telling God what should be done, and how and when, and then waiting for the expected result.

A little story, though often told, makes the point well. A man lived near a river at flood tide. Rain had poured down for days, and the water was rising fast. Ignoring all warnings to flee to higher ground, the man prayed for an angel to come and save him. As the water began to flood the yard, a fire truck drove up and the driver offered to take the man to higher ground. "No, thanks," said the man, "I am praying for an angel to come to get me." So the fire truck drove away. The water rose up to the porch and a rescue squad came by in a big motorboat, asking the man to get in and ride to safety. "No indeed," said the man, "I am expecting my angel any minute now." So the motorboat roared away. Finally the water reached the top of the house, and the man climbed to the roof. A helicopter hovered overhead and let down a rope ladder. But the man pushed the ladder away, looked at his watch, and said, "Certainly not! I am expecting an angel any time now." The helicopter flew away, the waters engulfed the house, and the man drowned. At the pearly gates the angry man confronted St. Peter: "I prayed hard. I believed. Why didn't God help me?" St. Peter answered, "First we sent you a fire truck, and then we sent you a motorboat, and then we sent you a helicopter. What were you expecting? An angel with wings?"

When Satan tempted Jesus to make God rescue him, Jesus answered, "Do not put the Lord your God to the test" (4:12). Rather than put God to the test, Christians may learn from Jesus and pray, "Lord, help me to give thanks for all you have already done. Help me to hear your voice and grasp your hand. Help me to keep trusting you no matter what may come. Amen."

QUESTIONS AND PRAYER

1. Satan's "big lie" is that evil is in control. When was the last time you heard the "big lie"?

2. When have you been tempted to test God? ("If I do such and so, then surely God will have to . . .")

3. What should Christians do when God does not act according to our plans?

Prayer: God of mercy, we often overlook what you are already doing for us and demand that you do something else instead. Forgive this unbelief. Help us to see your hand at work, providing, guiding, and healing. Amen.

Week 2: Teaching

J ESUS OFTEN TAUGHT IN STORIES called "parables," like the story of the widow and the judge. Other parables appear later in this journey through Lent with Luke. Some of Jesus' most powerful teachings, however, are not stories at all but short sayings—sayings that are one inch long and ten miles deep. Of these, the best known are Jesus' "beatitudes" or "blesseds." These appear in Luke 6 and are followed by several teachings in which Jesus encourages people to put his words to work in daily life. These and others of Jesus' teachings still bless, provoke, and inspire us today.

MONDAY

Read Luke 6:20-21. *"Blessed are you, . . . for yours is the kingdom of God"* (v. 20).

SOME BIBLES TRANSLATE the word *blessed* as "happy." So far, so good! Everyone wants to be happy. The "pursuit of happiness" is even enshrined by the Declaration of Independence. But Jesus' blessing is quite different from the pursuit of happiness. Indeed, the people Jesus singles out are those who do not seem to be happy at all: the poor, the hungry, and those who weep!

A natural reaction might be: "No, thanks." If poverty, hunger, and mourning are what it takes to receive God's blessing, most of us would rather pursue happiness in our own way. Some might think that the blessed are those who are rich, full, and surrounded by loved ones, and certainly these are gifts from God. But Jesus teaches people to look below the surface. Being comfortable and carefree is not what matters most in life.

To be blessed is to receive God's favor, to trust God's promises, and to live in God's presence—even in the most unhappy times. To be cursed is to be separated from God, which can happen even to those who enjoy wealth and ease.

Jesus' teachings turn natural expectations inside out. In Luke 6, he teaches that even the most painful situations, such as grief and poverty, may be occasions for blessing. "Blessed are you poor, for yours is the kingdom of God. Blessed are you who are hungry now, for you will be filled. Blessed are you who weep now, for you will laugh" (6:20-21). The people most likely to be shunned and avoided are the very people to whom Jesus promises God's blessing. And the situations people most want to avoid are the very situations in which God may bless them.

Sometimes well-meaning people treat the Beatitudes as ideals that must be achieved. This is a misunderstanding. Jesus is not pronouncing a standard to live up to, as though one must suffer to earn God's blessings. Jesus is not telling people to suffer this or that. Rather, he is speaking of what God does. He is promising God's compassion and help to those whom the world passes by.

God blesses people now. God walks with—and sometimes carries—people through the hardest times when no one else understands or cares. Psalm 139 says, "Where can I go from your spirit? Or where can I flee from your presence? If I take the wings of the morning and settle at the farthest limits of the sea, even there your hand shall lead me and your right hand shall hold me fast. If I say, 'Surely the darkness shall cover me, and the light around me become night'; even the darkness is not dark to you; the night is as bright as the day, for darkness is as light to you" (vv. 7, 9-11). Jesus himself promised, "I will not leave you orphaned; I am coming to you" (John 14:18). The comfort of the Holy Spirit is now, in the present moment, today.

The Beatitudes also point to the future. Those for whom life seems finished, who may seem to have nothing to look forward to, do indeed have a great future hope. Jesus says that those who are now hungry *will be filled* and those who now mourn *will be comforted.* Poverty, hunger, and sorrow are not God's final will. God shall bring in a better future, when "God himself will be with us, to wipe away every tear from our eyes. Death will be no more, mourning and crying and pain will be no more, for the first things have passed away" (Rev. 21:4).

Critics say that looking forward to heaven is just an escape hatch for those who cannot face reality. But the truth is, the hope of future blessing provides the endurance to face suffering and maintain trust in God. The promise of heaven inspires us to let go of our own "pursuit of happiness" and live on behalf of others, so that those who are hungry are filled and those who mourn are comforted and those who are poor finally have enough. The future hope makes the present moment blessed.

Questions and Prayer

1. If being comfortable and carefree is not what matters most in life, then what does?

2. Recall a time when God has blessed you, even in the midst of loss or difficulty.

Prayer: Lord God, help suffering people to find strength in you. Use me today to bless another human being. Amen.

Tuesday

Read Luke 6:22-23. *"Blessed are you when people hate you . . ."* (v. 22).

Martin Luther King Jr. once said that the person who "hasn't found something worth dying for isn't fit to live." For King, that "something worth dying for" was the dignity of human beings created in God's image—a dignity long denied to African Americans in the United States. King did not say that everyone has to suffer and die for a cause, but he did say that everyone needs to have something *worth* dying for. Jesus, who died on the cross, told his disciples that "a disciple is not above the teacher, but everyone who is fully qualified will be like the teacher" (6:40).

Many people think that church is all about being nice and expecting people to be nice in return. Controversy and conflict are to be avoided and the atmosphere kept safe and inoffensive. In such a controlled environment, the highest praise a pastor may receive is that he or she is very "nice." But along comes Jesus, saying, "Blessed are you when people hate you, exclude, revile, and defame you on account of the Son of Man" (6:22). To this most nice people reply, "Thanks for thinking of me, but if you don't mind, I'll pass on this one."

Jesus promises to bless those who face conflict "on account of the Son of Man"—those who, because of him, are despised, criticized, and slandered. Jesus tells his disciples to expect conflict if they follow him: "Woe to you when all speak well of you, for that is what their ancestors did to the false prophets" (6:26). Jesus' enemies accused him of treason, blasphemy, and madness; finally they succeeded in having him put to death.

Servants are not greater than their master. Early Christians, even when no formal or outright persecution was taking place, were disowned by families, shunned by neighbors, excluded from commerce and business, and expelled from synagogues. Because of the Lord's Supper, rumors spread that Christians were cannibals, eating human flesh and blood. It was thought that Christians could not possibly be good citizens, because they did not bow to Caesar. Many people feared that Christian refusal to worship pagan gods would bring disaster on the Roman Empire. For these and other offenses Christians were persecuted. In such times the faithful remembered Jesus' words: "Blessed are you when people hate you, and when they exclude you, revile you, defame you on account of the Son of Man. Rejoice in that day and leap for joy, for surely your reward is great in heaven, for that is what their ancestors did to the prophets" (6:22-23).

Christians suffer for Jesus' sake today, often in subtle ways but also in outright persecution. The Voice of the Martyrs (http://persecution.com) reports of a Pakistani Christian who was beaten for helping to show a film about Jesus. Six villagers in Bangladesh were beaten for becoming Christians. In North Vietnam, between eight thousand and ten thousand Christians have left their homes to avoid persecution. In China, Christians who are not members of the government-sanctioned "official" church can be jailed for preaching; many church buildings there have been destroyed, and Christian leaders have been beaten and jailed. In some parts of Indonesia, converts to Christianity are expelled from their villages. Meanwhile, Christians in safer parts of the world uphold their brothers and sisters in the faith with prayers, letters, advocacy, and other acts of love. Following Jesus is worth so much more than being "nice."

QUESTIONS AND PRAYER

1. Where do you see people who suffer "on account of the Son of Man"?

2. If you were accused of being a Christian, would there be any evidence to convict you?

Prayer: Lord Jesus, strengthen your suffering church with gifts of the Holy Spirit. Bless those who are persecuted because they bear your name. Inspire those who live in safety to help and support brothers and sisters who suffer for your name's sake. Amen.

WEDNESDAY

Read Luke 6:24-26. *"Woe to you who are rich, for you have received your consolation"* (v. 24).

AS JESUS' FAME SPREAD, people came from miles around to hear him. The crowd pressed in from all sides to touch Jesus; power came from him and many were healed. Jesus could have offered a general, one-size-fits-all message. Instead he treated people as individuals. Many needed healing. Some needed hope, comfort, or forgiveness. Still others needed food. And some, gripped by evil, needed release. Imagine looking at a crowd of people—at church, a football game, or anywhere—and knowing what each person most needed from God. Jesus did this and does this.

Jesus could have helped only the people whose needs were obvious and whose suffering was plain. But he also loved people who were secure in their wealth and status, people who seemed to need nothing from him. Their fine clothes and jewelry set them apart from the rough, common people. Their easy laughter mingled with the cries of the sick and the poor. Perhaps these idlers had heard that the famous teacher was in the neighborhood. This teacher might provide a diversion, a change of pace, a thought for the day; he might even perform a miracle. Jesus saw that these well-off people, every bit as much as the ragged and hungry folk, needed God. But wealth and pride masked their need. Like passengers in a climate-controlled car, they felt powerful and safe, untouched by heat or cold. Their inborn need for God had been numbed almost beyond feeling. They most likely enjoyed being "a cut above" the poor, unwashed folk who clamored for God's mercy.

Jesus might have ignored these smug people, leaving them untouched by God. But he was too great a teacher for that. The Teacher brings God's word to everyone. Jesus had just comforted the poor, hungry, and mourning, and he had promised God's blessing to those who were maligned for his sake. But these blessings are not for every situation. Jesus turns to the smug spectators and cries, "Woe to you who are rich, for you have received your consolation. Woe to you who are full now, for you will be hungry. Woe to you who are laughing now, for you will mourn and weep. Woe to you when all speak well of you, for that is what their ancestors did to the false prophets!" (6:24-26).

Woe means "sorrow." Jesus grieved over people who live and die without God. Jesus' cry of "woe" was his lament for the conceited people who thought they had it made. It was his distress over those who shut God out of their lives. *Woe* is also a warning. "Look out," Jesus says. "The things you have built your life on will crumble away. Watch out! Do you think you are better than the poor, the sick, and the captive? No one is fooled but you." Jesus sounds God's alarm over their lives: "Woe to you who have far to fall. Woe to you who look down on your brothers and sisters. Woe to you who don't need God and feel no pain for the world. You have your consolation now, but you will mourn and weep."

Like the prophets of old, Jesus warned the proud and complacent with the word *woe*. It would have been worse if he had passed them by in silence.

Questions and Prayer

1. How can people who seem comfortable and well-off be reached by the love of Christ?

2. Most people want to be blessed, but no one wants to experience woe. When do Jesus' warnings of woe most need to be spoken and heard?

Prayer: Lord Jesus, you could have passed by the proud and complacent people in silence. Instead you warned them, and you warn us: "Woe to you who are full now, for you will be empty." Help us to heed your warning and turn to you for life. Amen.

Thursday

Read Luke 6:27-36. *"Be merciful, just as your Father is merciful"* (v. 36).

"Love your enemies," Jesus said. "Do good to those who hate you." Jesus told his disciples to practice mercy in small ways every day. If someone curses us, respond with a blessing. Only God will see. Jesus said that if someone takes away our coat, we should give our shirt as well. When we lend money, we should not expect to be paid back. Our "reward" is living in God's mercy as God's children (6:35). Those who follow the Teacher will of course be taken advantage of by other people. Yet there is always the hope that God will use an act of mercy to change someone else's life. Showing mercy gives the Holy Spirit opportunity to work. When those who have received God's mercy in turn show mercy to others, God may use such a moment to lay hold of someone and say, "I love you, I call you, I claim you as my own."

Perhaps the great novelist Victor Hugo had Jesus' teaching in mind when he wrote *Les Misérables*, first published in 1862. Hugo tells of a young Frenchman, Jean Valjean, who had to support his sister's family by working as a tree pruner. One day the children cried for food, but Valjean had no work. Desperate for bread, he broke the window of a baker's shop and stole a loaf of bread to feed his family. The next day he was arrested and sentenced to five years hard labor as a galley slave—chained to a bench in a ship's hold, working the oars. Four times he tried to escape, and each time he was captured and his sentence lengthened. After serving nineteen years for stealing a loaf of bread, he was finally set free. But because he was an ex-convict, no one would give him work, food, or lodging. Valjean was free, but an outcast and a bitter man.

At last, Jean Valjean came to the home of a bishop, a devout man who lived simply and gave most of his money to the poor. The bishop gave Valjean a hot meal and a place to sleep. Jean offered to pay for lodging, but the bishop would not take his money, saying, "This is not my house; it is the house of Jesus Christ. . . . You are my brother." That night Valjean remembered the silver knives and forks they had used for supper and the silver candlesticks that lit the table. Little did he know that the bishop, having received the silver as a gift, did not feel easy about keeping it. Impelled by rage and bitterness for all the wrongs he had suffered, Valjean stole the silverware and vanished into the night.

The next morning, some officers dragged Jean Valjean and the stolen silver back to the bishop's house. But instead of crying, "Thief!" the bishop calmly said, "Ah! here you are! I am glad to see you. Why did you not carry them [the candlesticks] away with your forks and spoons?" Then the bishop told the men to let Valjean go, since he had given the silver to Valjean as a gift. Valjean was astonished when the bishop told him that he was free to go and that he should also take the silver candlesticks. The bishop charged him to use the silver items to become an honest man. "You no longer belong to evil, but to good. It is your soul that I buy from you; I withdraw it from [evil] thoughts, . . . and I give it to God." That act of mercy transformed Jean's life, and through peril and adventure, he tried to practice mercy.

Through the Gospel, Christ says, "I have bought your soul from the spirit of hate, and I give you to God. Therefore, show mercy to others as God shows mercy to you."

QUESTIONS AND PRAYER

1. Name a time in your life when you received mercy. How did this mercy change your life and your actions toward others?

2. Are you in a position to show mercy to another human being? What do you think God is calling you to do in this situation?

Prayer: O God, through the work of your son Jesus Christ, you have bought us from the spirit of hate and restored us to you. Inspire us, by the love of Christ, to show mercy to others as we ourselves have received mercy. Amen.

Friday

Read Luke 6:37-38. *"Do not judge, and you will not be judged . . ."* (v. 37).

Jesus' words, "Do not judge, and you will not be judged," are easily remembered, easily quoted, and easily twisted out of shape. For example, some people think that Jesus meant all judgments are bad, and therefore no one should judge another person. No one wants to be judgmental. Since we can never really know what it feels like to be in someone else's shoes—or so the argument goes—we should not condemn another person, even for actions that seem foolish, wrong, or hateful. How quickly people apply Jesus' words to any and every situation, as though it were some generic lotion or salve to be spread everywhere! Some may even think that Jesus' words, "Do not judge," mean that everything can be tolerated except intolerance. If that were true, no one could be held accountable for beliefs or actions, because it is not "nice" to make judgments. The trouble is, those who never make judgments will find themselves defenseless against evil.

Surely Jesus did not wish his followers to be naive about evil. Indeed, no one was more alert to the presence of evil than Jesus, and no one was less willing to compromise with it. Jesus' temptation in the wilderness shows us anything but bland acceptance and compromise. Jesus had to judge that Satan's voice was opposed to God's voice. And the more subtle Satan's tempting, the more discerning Jesus' judgment. Throughout his ministry, Jesus cast out demons, confronted hypocrites, exposed lies, forgave sins, and healed the sick. These are all forms of judgment in which Jesus sized up a situation and did the right thing at the right time. Nor did Jesus reserve judgment for extreme or exceptional cases. Indeed, he said, "Each tree is known by its fruit. No good tree bears bad fruit, nor again does a bad tree bear good fruit. Figs are not gathered from thorns, nor are grapes picked from a bramble bush" (7:43, 44). Jesus the teacher will also come again as our judge (21:36). Judgment has its place both in everyday life and in the grand scheme of things.

If the teaching "do not judge and you will not be judged" should not be spread like a salve over everything, how then should it be used? This teaching is best applied in situations of hypocrisy, self-righteousness, and injustice. The teaching is needed wherever people fail to see their own sin and focus on the sins of others. To make the remedy prescription strength, Jesus adds a warning: "Do not judge *and you will not be judged.*" God will judge people by the same standard they use to judge others.

Jesus knew how easy it is to see someone else's faults and how difficult it is to see one's own. Knowing that humor brings the truth to light, Jesus asked, "Why do you see the speck in your neighbor's eye, but do not see the log in your own eye? Or how can you say to your neighbor, 'Friend, let me take out the speck in your eye,' when you yourself do not see the log in your own eye? You hypocrite, first take the log out of your own eye, and then you will see clearly to take the speck out of your neighbor's eye" (6:41-42).

Jesus' saying, "Do not judge and you will not be judged," does not excuse people from using reason and discernment. Rather, it shows that all people alike are judged by God. Those who would make judgments must look at themselves first. This is a serious matter—yet Jesus' teaching overflows with promise: "Do not condemn, *and you will not be condemned.* Forgive, *and you will be forgiven.* Give, *and it will be given to you*—a good measure, pressed down and running over." Whether the last line of this teaching— "for the measure you give will be the measure you get back"— is promise or warning is, of course, a judgment call.

Questions and Prayer

1. What are some everyday situations in which people must make judgments?

2. Why is it so easy to see other people's faults and so difficult to see our own?

Prayer: Lord God, you created us with reason and gave us the capacity for making judgments. Help us to make good judgments that are pleasing in your sight. Forgive us for the times when we fail to see our own faults or imagine ourselves to be better than others. Amen.

Saturday

Read Luke 6:46-49. *"Why do you call me 'Lord, Lord,' and do not do what I tell you?"* (v. 46).

"IF YOU WANT TO LIVE another year on this planet," the doctor told Ben, "change your diet, exercise daily, and quit smoking." It was a wake-up call, Ben's last chance to do his body a favor before it was too late. Ben wrote down the doctor's advice. He read the literature the doctor provided, marking everything that applied to him. He even called the clinic to ask a few follow-up questions. The doctor hoped that Ben would change his ways while there was still time. Ben heard and understood the doctor's advice but did not put it into practice. And in less than twelve months, the doctor's warning came true. Ben's doctor could well have paraphrased Jesus' words: "Why do you call me 'Doctor, doctor,' and do not do what I tell you?"

Many people hear Jesus' words, agree with his teachings, perhaps even take notes, but go on living just the same as before. Hearing Jesus' teachings is not enough. Understanding them and saying yes is not enough. Those who take Jesus' teachings to heart seek to live by them every day.

To make the point, Jesus told this story: Once a wise builder dug deeply, laying the foundation of his house on a rock. Later a flood arose and the river burst against that house. But the house stood firm because it was built on a rock. So it is for those who hear Jesus' teachings and put them into practice. Meanwhile, another man built his house on sand. The storm came, the river rose, and the flood pushed against the house. The house fell with a great crash. So it goes for those who say, "Lord, Lord" but do not live by his Word.

Jesus does not promise that his followers will be spared from storms. In the parable, the flood batters the houses of both the wise and the foolish builders. Jesus does promise, however, that God's foundation stands firm when the storms come. God's love and mercy constitute the solid rock on which to build a godly life.

Imagine a brick or stone house. The house has a foundation, stones or bricks, and mortar to hold the stones together. Through his death and resurrection, Jesus has laid the foundation for a life with God. He gives us all the building blocks for life with God—mercy and blessing, warning and hope, love and truth. The mortar is a relationship with God and with other people. Most of Jesus' teachings in Luke 6—those very teachings that in 6:47 Jesus calls us to put into practice—are about living with other people. Every day God gives new opportunities to hear Jesus' words and act on them.

QUESTIONS AND PRAYER

1. When in your life have you received a "wake-up call"? How did you respond?

2. What are some of the "foundations" upon which people build their lives?

3. What opportunity does God give you today to put Jesus' teachings into practice?

Prayer: O Lord, you have promised that those who build on the firm foundation of faith in Christ will withstand the storms of life. Strengthen those who are caught in storms of grief, conflict, pain, or loss. Be a solid rock for them today. Amen.

SUNDAY

Read Luke 6:38; 9:12-14. *"Give, and it will be given to you"* (6:38).

ONE DAY A PIANO TEACHER GAVE HER STUDENT some new music, saying, "Come back next week and play this for me." The next week the student was able to tell the teacher several things about the piece: "It's in the key of G, with some complicated syncopation and a coda at the end." "Good," said the teacher, "now let me hear you play the piece." The student tried, but produced a noise that could barely be called music. "Didn't you practice it?" asked the teacher. "No," the student admitted. "I glanced at it once or twice but never really tried to play it."

Jesus, our teacher, wants us to put his words into practice: Mercy. Forgiveness. Generosity. In Luke 6, Jesus teaches generosity with money: "Give to everyone who begs from you"; with possessions: "From anyone who takes away your coat do not withhold even your shirt"; with patience: "If anyone strikes you on the cheek, offer the other also"; and with mercy: "Be merciful, as your Father is merciful." Mercy is not just an "accidental" or occasional note in the Christian life; it is the key signature for the whole symphony. When Jesus died on the cross, he poured out God's mercy. Nothing else in all the world can compare to this abundance, the generosity of his great outpouring of love.

Jesus teaches his followers to practice God's love daily. That's risky business: A person could get conned, taken advantage of, or burned out. Yet Jesus promises, "Give, and it will be given to you. A good measure, pressed down, shaken together, running over, will be put into your lap" (Luke 6:38). Jesus' words call to mind a sack of golden grain, packed so full that the ripe wheat spills out of the top. God promises to bless us in our giving. And God gives us the freedom to shape our lives and communities according to patterns of generosity or stinginess.

As mentioned, Jesus' teaching that "the measure you give will be the measure you get back" could be a warning or a promise. Not that there's always tit for tat in life, but over the long haul, people are blessed by showing mercy and generosity to others. Those who live out of scarcity, protecting their wallets and hearts, will find a stingy return on life's investment. Jesus is not teaching us to give so that we will be rewarded. He is saying that God's music is written in the key of mercy. Either we are playing our teacher's music or we are playing music other than God's.

Jesus said, "Give and it will be given you, a full measure, running over." Soon he gave his disciples a chance to put this teaching into practice. For Jesus taught not only in stories and sayings, but also by letting people try things out. Jesus sent his disciples to proclaim the kingdom of God, to cast out demons, and to heal the sick (9:1-6). They were to take nothing with them, relying only on God to provide. The disciples followed Jesus' directions and came back in wonder to tell Jesus of their adventures. As evening drew near, more people found Jesus and gathered around him. Many needed to be healed. The disciples thought that since there was nothing to eat and no place to sleep, Jesus ought to send the crowd away for the night. Surely these people could wait until tomorrow to ask for Jesus' help.

Then Jesus told the disciples, "You give them something to eat." Here was their chance to practice Jesus' teaching to "give and it will be given to you." But how? There were only five loaves and two fish to feed over five thousand people! But Jesus insisted, "Make them sit down in groups of about fifty each" (9:14). The disciples did so. Luke says that Jesus took the loaves and fish, blessed and divided them and gave them to the disciples to set before the crowd. Perhaps at this moment the disciples wondered if Jesus was out of touch. This just couldn't work! How strange must have been that moment when the disciples set the little meal before the great crowd. But by the grace of God, there was more than enough. When everyone had finished eating, there were twelve baskets of leftovers.

Jesus still teaches the practice of generosity. He does this by putting people in situations where they can give to others what they themselves receive from God. Jesus calls people to live out of abundance, not fearing that supplies will run out but trusting God to provide the increase.

Questions and Prayer

1. Jesus teaches people to be generous with money, possessions, patience, and mercy. With which of these is easiest for you to be generous? With which the most difficult?

2. What would it mean for you to "live out of abundance" rather than to "live out of scarcity"?

Prayer: Holy Spirit, inspire us to share freely with others what we ourselves have received. Where we are lacking in wealth, courage, wisdom, or love, help us to trust in you to provide the increase. Amen.

WEEK 3: HEALING

JESUS' GREAT POWER TO HEAL shines in Luke's Gospel. Jesus gives new life to those who seem to be beyond help. To heal people, Jesus sometimes broke rules and customs. He also awakened faith in those whom he healed, changing their souls as well as their bodies. Complete healing restores the whole person, body and soul, and mends broken communities.

MONDAY

Read Luke 7:1-10. *"Only speak the word, and let my servant be healed"* (v. 7).

IN CAPERNAUM, BY THE SEA OF GALILEE, Jesus was teaching people and healing the sick. In that region lived a Roman centurion, an officer commanding one hundred soldiers. The Romans placed such commanders with their soldiers throughout the sprawling empire to keep local peoples under control. In addition to functioning as a military commander, a centurion might also act as a diplomat, administrator, or police chief.

The centurion was equal to the task. He combined the right skills with a winning attitude. If he were alive today, he could write a best-seller on self-help or on the keys to successful management. If he were alive today, he would be called "proactive." Rather than sit around waiting for things to happen, he made things happen. Always sending messages to the right people at the right time, he would have loved fax machines, e-mail, and cell phones.

The centurion looked for win-win situations. For example, he helped the people of Capernaum to build a synagogue for worship. Perhaps this Roman officer admired the Jewish faith and wanted to support it. Or perhaps he, like some enlightened rulers, knew that people are easier to govern if they are allowed certain freedoms, such as worship. Whatever the centurion's motives, helping the people build their synagogue was a win-win situation. If he did the locals a favor, they would cooperate with the Roman occupation. The people would have a synagogue, and his own job would be easier. If challenged, the centurion could always use force, but he preferred a more subtle approach.

Finally, the centurion was interdependent in his relationships. People depended on him and he depended on people. He carried out orders from his superiors and he gave orders to those below him in the chain of command. Yet his subordinates were not just cogs in Rome's imperial machine. They were people. When a favorite servant of his was at the point of death, the centurion could have replaced him, just as he would replace a broken wheel on his chariot. But the centurion knew that people are not just interchangeable parts. This servant was a highly valued member of the centurion's household—someone to be saved, not just replaced.

This valued servant was dying. And his impending death brought the centurion to a place where self-help is no help at all. True, the centurion's soldiers followed his orders, and his servants obeyed his commands. But here he was, a man of many gifts and powers, a man who could usually help himself, at a place where what mattered most was beyond his control. Life, the gift he wanted most for his valued servant, was not his to give. Self-help is good as far as it goes, but the centurion knew the limits of his own powers. He had heard about Jesus, so he sent some Jewish elders to ask Jesus to heal his slave.

35

The Jewish elders, grateful for their new synagogue, appealed to Jesus: "He deserves your help, for he loves our people and he built our synagogue for us" (7:4-5). Jesus went with the elders. As they approached the house, the centurion sent friends to say to him, "Lord, do not trouble yourself, for I do not deserve to have you in my house . . . just say the word and let my servant be healed. For I also am a man under authority, with soldiers under me; and I say to one, 'Go,' and he goes, and to another, 'Come,' and he comes, and to my slave, 'Do this,' and he does it." Amazed by these words, Jesus turns to the crowd and says, "I tell you, not even in Israel have I found such faith" (vv. 8-9). The Roman officer's messengers return to the house to find the servant restored to health.

The centurion could have written the book on self-help for his own time and place. Yet he saw his own limits. Seeing his servant dying, he cried out, "I can no longer help myself." Self-help did not exempt him from the need for God's help. Rather than ask Jesus to return a favor ("I helped your people build a place of worship, so now you can help me"), he asked Jesus to show mercy. The centurion trusted himself and his household completely to Jesus, who alone has authority to give life.

QUESTIONS AND PRAYER

1. What is the place of self-help strategies in the Christian life? Have any particular self-help books, speakers, or authors been important for you?

2. The Roman centurion understood authority and used his own authority well. Over what has God given you authority? Under whose authority do you live and work?

Prayer: God, we thank you for the many ways in which we can improve our own lives and the lives of others. Help us to make the best of the opportunities you give us, but at the same time, help us to recognize our complete dependence upon you. Amen.

TUESDAY

Read Luke 8:26-33. *The demons came out of the man and entered the swine, and the herd rushed down the steep bank into the lake and was drowned* (v. 33).

EVERY COMMUNITY SHOULD HAVE A HERD OF PIGS into which demons can be cast. A raucous herd of muddy pigs would be a good home for evils that move in and try to take over individuals, families, and communities. If only anger, fatalism and unbelief, poverty, hatred and greed, and other things that plague people could take up residence elsewhere, leaving everyone free and "in their right minds."

Such an imagining seems wild and superstitious, of course. Perhaps it is a good thing that people seldom speak of demons. Many years ago, when diseases such as epilepsy were thought to be caused by evil spirits, sufferers were blamed for their problems and had to carry the extra burden of stigma. Often this meant being shut out of the community at the very time when support was most needed.

Clearly, we've come a long way in our understanding of diseases and evil, and it would seem neighborhood pig herds aren't needed. But many people think there is *no* evil around or within. For them the need for Jesus' prayer, "Deliver us from evil," remains hidden, its power untapped. Throughout Luke's Gospel, Jesus demonstrated his power to "deliver us from evil," a power that was and is every bit as important as his power to heal people from disease. Everywhere he went, Jesus healed the sick and cast out demons. When evil spirits took over a person's life, that person needed someone stronger than the demons to confront and banish the possessing power.

Today there are times when a "possessing power" must be named and confronted before it can be defeated. In some cases of chemical dependency, for example, a person's family, friends, and coworkers may join in an intervention in which the dependent person is confronted with evidence of his or her addiction. Although this is just the beginning of healing, the intervention itself, confronting and naming the addiction, can be a life-changing moment. Without the intervention, where addiction is brought into the open, healing will never happen. Addiction is but one example of a "power" that can take over people's lives, of course.

"Delivering from evil" is precisely what Jesus did for the wild, naked man who lived among the tombs. Others had tried to contain this man by chaining him up, but tumultuous powers burst even the strongest shackles, driving the afflicted man into the wilderness. Then one day the demons and their unwilling host came face-to-face with Jesus. The afflicted man fell down and shouted at the top of his voice, "What have you to do with me, Jesus, son of the Most High God? I beg you, do not torment me!" (8:28). The evil spirits knew Jesus' power to be stronger than their own. If they acknowledged that power, perhaps Jesus would pass on by. But Jesus would have none of it; he was going to intervene. "What is your name?" Jesus asked. They answered, "Legion," for many demons had entered the man. They begged Jesus not to order them back to "the abyss" (vv. 30, 31).

There on the hillside by the Sea of Galilee, a large herd of swine was feeding. The demons begged Jesus to let them enter these swine. Perhaps to spare the man from yet more agony, Jesus granted their request. The demons came out of the man and entered the swine. Shrill squeals and wild grunts filled the air the as the swine stampeded down the steep bank, plunged into the lake, and drowned.

Pastel colors will not paint this picture. Its hues are bold, loud, and harsh. But the picture of the swine stampeding over the cliff proclaims Jesus' power and authority over every other power. Christ can free people from bondage, restoring them to life and health. Indeed, the man in this story was found clothed and in his right mind, sitting at Jesus' feet.

QUESTIONS AND PRAYER

1. If you could get rid of one personal or community "demon," what would it be?

2. What can Christians learn about spiritual powers from recovery movements such as Alcoholics Anonymous?

3. When in your life has the prayer "deliver us from evil" been most urgently needed?

Prayer: Lord, deliver us from evil. Give us strength and confidence in your power to set us free, forgive us, and make us alive in Christ. Yours is the final victory over sin, death, and every power that opposes your loving will. Amen.

Wednesday

Read Luke 8:34-39. *The people came out to see what had happened . . .* (v. 35).

THE WILD MAN OF THE TOMBS was healed! His tormentors had been evicted and the man was now free to live a normal life. The very person who once was feared and chained up like an animal was now, astonishingly, just like everyone else! In response to this miraculous healing, people should have knelt down to worship Jesus. After all, the Healer had just won a battle with evil, liberating a man whom everyone assumed was forever captive. People should have been relieved that the wild man of the tombs would no longer frighten them or their children. There should have been a neighborhood party for Jesus, or at least a dinner invitation.

But that is not what happened. The swineherds, who had seen their livelihood plunge headlong into the sea, ran off to tell everyone in town. People came rushing to see Jesus, and they found the man whom the demons had plagued sitting clothed and in his right mind at Jesus' feet. Luke says that they "were afraid." Jesus was more powerful than anyone had guessed! No one had room for a person as big as Jesus. And besides, everyone had been sure that the wild man of the tombs was beyond hope. Jesus changed all that. The whole community would now have to change to make room for the newly healed man among them.

Luke does not describe exactly what people were saying, but it is not hard to imagine. "How will we make a living now that he's drowned our pigs?" the swineherds grumble. "This neighborhood just isn't safe with Jesus around," the townspeople complain. "We feared the wild man, but at least he stayed out of sight most of the time. Must we now see him every day and accept him as one of us?" the neighbors worry. "If Jesus stays around here much longer, there is no telling what he will do next." The people ask Jesus to go away because they are "seized with great fear" (8:37).

As Jesus gets back into the boat to return across the lake, the healed man begs to go with him. How great it would be for this healed man to follow Jesus, leaving behind the years of anguish and humiliation in his home town! Yet Jesus tells him, "Return to your home, and declare how much God has done for you" (8:39). The man does so, telling Jesus' deeds throughout the city.

According to Luke, the people responded to Jesus' work of healing in two ways: fear and gratitude. The townspeople were afraid of Jesus, and probably continued to fear the healed man. They may also have feared that if Jesus stayed in their town, other valuable livestock might be destroyed. In contrast to fear, the healed man's response was gratitude. Now set free, he shone with health and thankfulness. Luke describes him as "clothed and in his right mind, sitting at the feet of Jesus" (8:35). In a physical sense, he was clothed, no longer living like an animal among the tombs. But in a spiritual sense, he was clothed with the grace of God. He was now in his right mind, free to serve and praise God. He was in his "right mind" because he recognized Jesus and thanked him. Everywhere he went, he told people what Jesus had done for him, and although he may never have seen the Healer again, he lived the rest of his life in grateful obedience.

QUESTIONS AND PRAYER

1. Suppose a person recovers from a long-term problem. How could this recovery affect the person's family, friends, and coworkers? In what ways might *they* need to change?

2. Why do some people respond to Jesus with fear, while others respond with gratitude?

Prayer: Lord, give us courage to change along with the people you heal. May the Holy Spirit give the gift of gratitude to all who experience your saving help. Amen.

THURSDAY

Read Luke 8:43-48. *Then Jesus asked, "Who touched me?"* (v. 45).

THE MAN WHOM JESUS RESTORED "to his right mind" (8:35) went and told everyone what Jesus had done for him. While he went public with his story, another person, across the Sea of Galilee, bore a private anguish. For twelve years she had suffered from heavy bleeding. Despite having spent all her savings on physicians who could not cure her, she clung to the hope that somehow she would be healed. Not only her money but her strength was gone as she faced the prospect of death every day. Such suffering was heavy enough, but adding to it was the ritual law declaring that a woman with an irregular discharge of blood was considered "unclean" or contaminated (Lev. 15:25-27). Another person touching such a woman, or her bed, chair, or other objects of daily use, would also become unclean. Today such beliefs are easily shrugged off, yet people still try to protect themselves by isolating the sufferer.

In spite of it all, this woman found the courage to venture out into a crowd. It may have taken her last ounce of strength. How much easier it would have been to stay home and rest, rather than risk bringing on another episode of bleeding. Nevertheless, she left her home in search of Jesus. Although she saw him surrounded by a crowd, the woman managed to work her way toward him, coming up from behind. She did not speak to him, perhaps fearing that a great spiritual leader such as Jesus would sense her "uncleanness" and reject her. She may have had no strategy at all—just a wordless, desperate plea. She touched the fringe of his garment and her bleeding stopped.

Then Jesus said, "Who touched me?" In a crowd where people were constantly pushing and jostling to get close to Jesus, it was a strange thing to ask. Peter said, "Master, the crowds surround you and press in on you." But Jesus insisted, "Someone touched me, for I noticed that power had gone out from me" (Luke 8:45-46).

Sometimes Christians are troubled by Jesus' question. Didn't he know who touched him? Doesn't Jesus know everything? Whether or not he knew specifically who it was that touched him, Jesus knew that the person in question needed to come out into the open. Faith may be personal, but it is also public. So Jesus asked, "Someone touched me—who is it?"

The woman could not remain hidden. She would have to make herself known. Trembling, she fell down before Jesus. In the presence of all the people in the crowd, she told Jesus why she had touched him and how she had been healed. Luke does not say if neighbors recognized this woman or if she was unknown to the crowd. Either way, her story must have shocked those in the crowd. She might well have expected everyone to draw back from her. She might well have expected Jesus to reject her. For although she was now healed, she had yet to go through purification rites. She had not followed the rules. How could she, an unclean woman, dare to touch a great religious leader? Would Jesus now be considered unclean because of her? The woman's deed was like theft, taking Jesus' healing power without payment or permission. In those times, she could have expected people to shout at her, "Thief!" "Outcast!" "Dog!"

But not Jesus. He called her "daughter," a term of endearment. Child of God, daughter of Israel, beloved. "Daughter," he said, "your faith has made you well. Go in peace" (8:48). Jesus had already healed her. And now he mended her relationship with God and with her community. Her touch did not make him unclean; rather, his touch made her whole.

Questions and Prayer

1. Name one specific time when you have avoided contact with someone who is suffering. What could you do differently next time?

2. Why do you think Jesus asked, "Who touched me?"

Prayer: Gracious God, we remember the people who are isolated by grief, depression, or physical suffering. Bless, help, and heal them with your touch. Move us to break through someone else's isolation with a word or an act of grace. Amen.

Friday

Read Luke 17:11-19. *Then one of them, when he saw that he was healed, turned back, praising God with a loud voice* (v. 15).

ON HIS WAY TO JERUSALEM, Jesus passed between Samaria and Galilee. Here fertile valleys thread their way between terraced hills dotted with olive trees. As Jesus entered a village, ten lepers called to him. Because their skin disease was thought to be contagious, they lived separately from family and friends, outcasts from the village. They did not come near Jesus but shouted from a distance, "Jesus, Master, have mercy on us" (7:13).

On this desperate plea the ten lepers had a great deal riding: their health and their hope of returning to friends and family. But Jesus made no show of miracle working. He simply told them to show themselves to the priests, who would examine them and verify that they were "clean" of disease. Then these ten "cleansed" people could be officially restored to their community (Lev. 13:2, 3; 14:2-32). But before all this could happen, the ten would have to trust Jesus. He asked them to go and see the priests before they had actually been healed. They may have wondered why Jesus did not heal them first and then send them to the priests for a clean bill of health, but they obeyed Jesus, and "as they went, they were made clean" (Luke 17:14). Nine of the ten continued on their way to the priests. One man, overcome with gratitude, turned back. Shouting praises to God with a loud voice, he fell down before Jesus and thanked him.

Luke makes a point of saying that the grateful man who came back to Jesus was a Samaritan and a foreigner. Jews and Samaritans had much in common, but Samaritans worshiped in ways significantly different from the standard faith and practice of Israel. For example, they worshiped on Mt. Gerizim, not at the temple in Jerusalem (John 4:20). When it came to religion, Samaritans did not conform. This particular Samaritan was a case in point: rather than follow directions ("go and show yourselves to the priests"), he came back and threw himself at Jesus' feet. He poured out his gratitude, praising God for the gift of healing. Compared to the response of the other nine, this man's outburst was something like the person who shouts "amen" and "hallelujah" in liturgical worship service when no such response is printed in the bulletin.

Luke does not describe the expression on Jesus' face or the tone of Jesus' voice when the grateful man returned. It seems likely, however, that Jesus was deeply moved by this man's grateful praises. "Were not ten lepers cleansed?" Jesus asked. "Yet only this foreigner returned to praise God!" Jesus told the man, "Get up and go on your way; your faith has made you well" (Luke 17:19).

Gratitude is a sign of spiritual health, which is every bit as important as physical health. When people recover from an illness or survive a surgery, when a broken bone mends and the cast comes off, when a relationship is restored, when depression lifts, when addiction's grip is loosened, people are often moved to praise God. Of course, it is possible to enjoy physical health—indeed, many people enjoy a lifetime of health—without gratitude to God. It is also possible to be grateful to God despite physical suffering. By faith Christians look forward to a day when everyone will praise God and, like this healed man, be completely whole in body and soul.

Questions and Prayer

1. Why do you think Jesus did not heal the ten lepers first and then tell them to go and see the priests?

2. The nine healed lepers who went to show themselves to the priests were following Jesus' orders. Why, then, did Jesus praise only the one who returned to give thanks?

Prayer: Holy Spirit, you give the gifts of gratitude and joy. May we today, even in mourning or suffering, find a glimmer of light in God's mercies—past, present, or future. Amen.

Saturday

Read Luke 18:35-43. They told him, *"Jesus of Nazareth is passing by"* (v. 37).

By the roadside, just outside of Jericho, sat a beggar. Though he was blind, he knew the road as well as anyone—he knew it by sound. His ears told him the daily rhythms along the road between Jerusalem and Jericho, the traffic of footsteps and hoof beats, the bleating of sheep and goats on their way to market. Sometimes Herod himself traveled this road on his way to his luxurious winter capital. The blind man could tell by the sounds of horses and wheels when Herod and his court were passing by.

This blind man was one of many who waited at every town's edge, hoping that someone would spare him a coin or a morsel of food. A beggar could become a fixed part of the scenery, holding forth at the very same spot for years on end. There was nowhere to go and nothing to do but listen and wait and beg.

One day the beggar heard a crowd going by. It was not Herod—for there was no fanfare, no chariot wheels, no horses. This crowd sounded like common people, but why had they gathered? People were filling the road, gathering in front of the blind man. He could tell from the excited voices that something unusual was happening. Then someone told him that Jesus of Nazareth was passing by.

Now the blind man, after years of waiting and listening, shouted, "Jesus, Son of David, have mercy on me!" (Luke 18:38). "Son of David" is a royal title, acknowledging Jesus as a descendant of the great King David. Somehow this blind beggar knew what many others could not see—that Jesus was the King. This was no time to ask for a coin or a piece of bread; it was time to ask for something much bigger, something far greater than he had ever dared request before. "Jesus, Son of David," he cried out, "have mercy on me!"

But his shouting annoyed some people. "Be quiet," they hissed. This beggar was a nuisance, spoiling the parade with his yelling. But the blind beggar shouted all the more, "Son of David, have mercy on me!"

Jesus stopped. The crowd stopped with him. This noisy beggar, who did not have enough sense to keep quiet in the presence of a king, had brought the whole procession to a halt. And with kingly authority Jesus ordered that the beggar be brought to him (18:40). The man was obviously blind, but Jesus asked, "What do you want me to do for you?"

The beggar could have done what people so often do in the presence of God: He could have asked for too little and shielded himself against disappointment if the request was not granted. But the beggar, though physically blind, believed or at least hoped that Jesus could heal him. Why ask for a handout when you could ask for your whole life to be changed? "Lord," he said, "let me see again." It was a daring request, bold as brass. He had not let the moment slip. Jesus said to him, "Receive your sight. Your faith has saved you" (Luke 18:41, 42). Immediately the man received his sight and followed Jesus, glorifying God. And when the people saw it, they all praised God. Their eyes were opened too; never before had they seen anything like this.

QUESTIONS AND PRAYER

1. In what ways did the beggar, though blind, "see" Jesus?

2. How was the crowd helped to "see" by the beggar's encounter with Jesus?

Prayer: Lord Jesus, you came to open the eyes of the blind, to declare liberty to the captives, and to set free those who are bound. Please bring healing to those in our lives we name before you. You know their needs, and you know ours. Amen.

SUNDAY

Read Luke 19:1–10. *"Today salvation has come to this house . . ."* (v. 9).

SOME THINGS ESSENTIAL TO LIFE are not covered by insurance—such as a new pair of glasses, a change of heart, or a conversion. What Zacchaeus needed would cost him a lot, but it would be pointless to submit a claim form for it. Perhaps the story of Zacchaeus's change of heart does not qualify as a healing story. After all, this man was not cleansed of leprosy. He was not healed of persistent bleeding, set free from demon possession, or given his sight for the first time. But he was healed of an equally deadly disease, a malady so common that most people regard it as normal. Zacchaeus was healed of greed.

Zacchaeus was a rich tax collector. He lived in Jericho, a town abundant with goods to be taxed because it was on a main trading route. Luke describes Zacchaeus as "a chief tax collector, and rich" (19:2). Like a jackal feeding on the leftovers of a lion's meal, Zacchaeus was well fed by Rome's occupation of Israel. No wonder his countrymen regarded him as a "sinner," a traitor, a scavenger. And yet, some light flickered within his shadowy soul. When Jesus was passing through Jericho, Zacchaeus felt compelled to see Jesus. He could not see over the heads of the crowd, so he climbed up into a tree. As Jesus passed by, he said to Zacchaeus, "Hurry and come down; for I must stay at your house today" (19:5). Zacchaeus quickly climbed down from the tree and received Jesus joyfully.

The people who saw it grumbled, "Jesus will be the guest of a sinner!" (19:7). Jesus, of all people, should have known that eating with a sinner such as Zacchaeus would damage his reputation. To see Jesus breaking bread with a tax collector would be worse than seeing a dove eating with vultures. Surely the taint of corruption would rub off on Jesus and stain his public image. The tax collector's greed, his wealth, his open support of the hated Roman occupation—all of these were worse than bleeding, worse than blindness, worse than leprosy, as far as the people were concerned. And who could blame them?

But Jesus came to Zacchaeus, and the tax collector changed. He said to Jesus, "I will give half of my goods to the poor, and if I have cheated anyone of anything, I will give back four times that amount" (19:8). Jesus had healed this man of greed. As surely as the blind beggar had received his physical sight, the tax collector received from Jesus a new moral sight. Zacchaeus no longer saw his neighbors as people to be exploited but as people to be treated justly. For Zacchaeus, healing meant making restitution to those whom he had cheated. Healing meant that from that day forward he would treat people differently. And Jesus said, "Today salvation has come to this house, since he also is a son of Abraham" (19:9). Even this despised tax collector was a child of God, a member of the Lord's family. Salvation—making whole, making well, restoring of a life to God—came to Zacchaeus's house that day. For Jesus came to seek and to save the lost.

Questions and Prayer

1. Have you ever needed "healing" in your life from something that was not a physical problem?

2. Jesus said, "The Son of Man came to seek and save the lost." What does this mean to you?

Prayer: Thank you, Lord Jesus, for not caring what others thought of you. Thank you for eating with tax collectors and sinners. Thank you for healing people and changing their lives. May we rejoice with you and with all whom you seek and save. Amen.

WEEK 4: FORGIVING 🌿

ORGIVENESS IS A FORM OF HEALING. It is a powerful gift from God that heals those who forgive and those who are forgiven. Jesus taught his followers to practice this gift for others and to receive it gladly for themselves.

MONDAY

Read Luke 5:17-26. *"Which is easier, to say, 'Your sins are forgiven you,' or to say, 'Stand up and walk'?"* (v. 23).

PEOPLE WERE PACKED so tightly inside the house where Jesus was, and all around it, that getting close to him seemed about as likely as finding a parking place in Manhattan. A group of people carried a man to the edge of the crowd. "There must be a way to get to Jesus," friends of the paralyzed man exclaimed. Wanting Jesus to heal their friend and having carried him this far, they were not about to turn back. "We'll have to go in through the roof!" The house had a flat roof made of tiles. Somehow the men managed to get their friend up there. Then they started removing tiles. Inside the crowded house, dust and sand began sifting down as the men made an opening in the roof. Sunlight streamed in. When the opening was big enough, the men lowered their friend down on his pallet, right in front of Jesus.

Looking down through the opening in the roof and seeing their paralyzed friend lying at Jesus' feet, these men expected a miracle. But Jesus did not do what they wanted or expected, at least not on cue. Instead Jesus said to the paralyzed man, "Friend, your sins are forgiven you!" (5:20). Watching the scene through the opening in the roof, the man's friends may have been disappointed. Had they muscled their way through the crowd, lifted their friend to the top of the house, and made a hole in the roof just to have their friend's sins forgiven? Surely Jesus could see the *real* problem! What was a word of forgiveness, compared with the heroic efforts of these men? To them it most likely seemed that Jesus did too little.

But Jesus had done too much, as far as the scribes and Pharisees in the house were concerned. By speaking the words "your sins are forgiven," Jesus did something only God should do. For a man like Jesus to put himself in the place of God was blasphemy. Only God can forgive sins! If Jesus had healed the man, these religious leaders could have accepted a miracle and perhaps even rejoiced in it. But Jesus had stepped over the line.

Perceiving their outrage, Jesus asked them, "Which is easier, to say, 'Your sins are forgiven,' or to say, 'Stand up and walk'?" But so that you may know that the Son of Man has authority on earth to forgive sins . . ." (5:24). Then Jesus spoke to the paralyzed man, saying, "Stand up and take your bed and go home." Immediately the man stood up and took up his pallet. In awe, the crowd pressed back to let the healed man pass through. Everyone was amazed. They said, "We have seen strange things today" (v. 26).

Jesus heals both body and spirit. In this story, Jesus holds the forgiveness of sins to be even greater than physical healing. Most people tend to see it the other way around. Forgiving sins may seem like mere words, something rather ordinary, but this attitude only shows how easy it is to underestimate sin's hold on people. Sin paralyzes the spirit, blinds the heart, and afflicts people with unbelief. This, in turn, cuts people off from God and from each other, just as surely as a disease may isolate a sufferer.

When Jesus forgives sins, he renews people from within and restores them to God and to each other. The Pharisees underestimated Jesus' power and authority. In this much, however, they were right: Forgiving sins is "a God thing."

Questions and Prayer

1. Name one person for whom you could pray (or are already praying). What do you pray for on behalf of this person?

2. In the story from Luke 5:17-26, why did Jesus first forgive the man's sins rather than heal him right away?

Prayer: O God, through your son Jesus Christ you forgive sins. You can heal us from sin that separates us from you and from each other. We thank and praise you for the great gift of healing that comes through forgiveness. Amen.

Tuesday

Read Luke 7:36-50. *"Her sins, which were many, have been forgiven; hence she has shown great love"* (v. 47).

A MIRROR GIVES A TRUE REFLECTION of each person who looks into it. The very same mirror may show opposite things, depending on whose face it reflects. Many of Jesus' words and deeds are like mirrors, reflecting a person's relationship with God. The very same Gospel story may convict or comfort, depending on who hears the story.

Take, for example, the time when Jesus was invited to a meal at the home of a Pharisee named Simon. A woman had followed

Jesus there. This woman had a bad reputation, yet she showed great love and devotion to Jesus. She anointed his feet with fragrant oil, and then bathed his feet with her tears and dried them with her hair. Heedless that her display upset the other guests, she continued kissing Jesus' feet and covering them with the ointment. The custom of bathing a guest's feet was not unusual in a culture where people traveled hot, dusty roads on foot, but this woman's weeping and kissing Jesus' feet, and then drying his feet with her hair, was a bit over the top. What's more, it continued long enough to make the host and the other guests uncomfortable.

Simon, the Pharisee who invited Jesus, muttered to himself, "If Jesus were a prophet, he would know what kind of woman this is who is touching him, and that she is a sinner!" (7:39). Jesus' acceptance of this woman's tribute made it more and more difficult for Simon to accept Jesus. Perhaps inviting Jesus to his home has been a big mistake. The whole situation was proving most embarrassing!

Jesus knew what Simon was thinking. "Simon," Jesus said, "I have something to say to you." Then Jesus told a parable. This parable was like a mirror in which Simon and every guest could see his or her own reflection. The story concerned a lender who had two debtors. One debtor owed five hundred days' wages, the other owed fifty. Neither one could pay, so the moneylender canceled the debts of both. "Now," Jesus said, "which debtor will love the moneylender more?" Simon replied, "I suppose the one for whom he canceled the greater debt." Jesus answered, "You have judged rightly" (7:41, 42).

Then Jesus asked Simon to look at the woman—yes, rather than try to ignore her, to *look* at her. "I entered your house, Simon," Jesus said. "You gave me no water for my feet, but she has washed my feet with her tears and dried them with her hair. You did not greet me with a kiss, but she has not stopped kissing my feet since I came in. You did not anoint my head with oil, but she has lavished this ointment upon my feet." And then Jesus said something guaranteed to offend polite company: "Therefore, I tell you, her sins, which were many, have been forgiven, hence she has shown great love. But the one to whom little is forgiven, loves little" (7:47).

Everyone was astonished: "Who is this who even forgives sins?" Jesus did not bother to smooth their ruffled feathers. Instead he spoke to the woman, the uninvited guest: "Your faith has saved you; go in peace" (7:50). To this day, his message is a mirror into which each person can look: Whoever has been forgiven much, loves much, and whoever has been forgiven little, loves little.

QUESTIONS AND PRAYER

1. What is your response to Jesus' message: "Whoever has been forgiven little, loves little; whoever has been forgiven much, loves much"?

2. The woman in the story washed Jesus' feet with her tears and dried them with her hair. Why do you think Jesus accepted this gesture that offended others?

Prayer: Lord God, in the mirror of your Word, you show us our need to forgive and to be forgiven. Thank you for your abundant grace. May we receive it with joy. Amen.

Wednesday

Read Luke 11:4: *"And forgive us our sins, for we ourselves forgive everyone who is indebted to us."*

ONCE A LITTLE GIRL COMPLAINED OF PAIN in her ear. Asked which ear was hurting, she pointed first to her left ear, and then to her right, and then to both ears at once. A doctor took the child's temperature and examined her ears. "Her fever is 101," pronounced the doctor, "and both ears are infected." Once the problem was diagnosed, something could be done to help the girl. The doctor began to write a prescription for medicine to stop the pain, tame the fever, and fight the infection. Well and good. But wouldn't it be strange if the doctor said, "I will prescribe medication that will treat the left ear and leave the right one alone"? Of course the parents would object: "That makes no sense! A total cure is needed, not half a cure. We must treat both sides."

Like the little girl with the double ear infection, people have a two-sided illness. The malady is sin, rebellion against God. It is two sided because we ourselves sin and we are sinned against. The cure is two sided as well: We need to be forgiven and we need to forgive others. Just as a simple ear infection can cause damage if it is left untreated, so can sin, if left untreated, damage our relationship with God and with other people. The good news is, God offers healing through repentance and forgiveness. The bad news is, most people settle for a halfway treatment.

People who receive forgiveness often refuse to forgive others, and then they wonder why healing does not come! Jesus, the Great Physician, loves people too much to prescribe a halfway remedy for sin. That is why he taught us to pray: "Forgive us our sins *as we forgive those who sin against us."* This is the double-sided cure for those who sin and are sinned against—in other words, everyone.

Sometimes infections fester undetected. This happens when people cling to the wrong that has been done to them and refuse to let it go. The wrongs done to us are every bit as lethal, every bit as toxic, as the wrongs we have committed. Refusal to forgive others works like a hidden infection, spreading poison throughout one's life. Knowing just how bad this infection can get, Jesus prescribes grace through this prayer: "Forgive us our sins as we forgive those who sin against us." His grace can heal both the sins we commit and the sins committed against us. It does us no good to treat one side of the problem without treating the other. Forgiveness is God's prescription.

Many prescriptions come with a warning label, and so does God's: If only one side of the problem is treated, the medicine will not work properly. Martin Luther wrote in the Large Catechism, "If you do not forgive, do not think that God forgives you. But if you forgive, you have the comfort and assurance that you are forgiven in heaven. God forgives freely, out of pure grace, but he has set up this condition to strengthen us and assure us of his promise" (*The Book of Concord,* 433). God knows we need to receive forgiveness and also to give it. That is why Jesus gives the strongest possible prescription in the Lord's Prayer: "Forgive us our sins, as we forgive those who sin against us." God wants us to hear the music of grace clearly, with both ears.

QUESTIONS AND PRAYER

1. When you forgive someone else, what do you give up?

2. When you forgive someone else, what do you gain?

3. Do you see yourself both sinning and sinned against? Why or why not?

Prayer: Lord, you taught your disciples to pray: "Forgive us our sins, as we forgive those who sin against us." Help me to pray both sides of that prayer today. Amen.

THURSDAY

Read Luke 17:3-5. *"You must rebuke; . . . you must forgive"* (v. 3).

I ONCE RECEIVED AN UNUSUAL PRESENT from a friend who is a Civil War buff. The gift was a packet containing several bullets from Civil War battlefields. These heavy lead projectiles once flew thick as hailstones. Some bullets fell harmlessly to the ground, to be found decades later by souvenir hunters with metal detectors or dug up by squirrels. Some bullets lodged in trees, buildings, or fences. Countless others hit their mark—the Union or Confederate soldiers. Hundreds of thousands of soldiers died from these bullet wounds; untold others were wounded. Some wounded soldiers had the bullets removed by army surgeons. These men, though scarred and often severely injured, could now begin to heal. Still other men lived out their years with lead bullets in their bodies, the lead spreading its slow poison long after the war was over.

Something like this happens when people carry with them the injuries they have suffered at the hand of others. The "bullet" continues to do harm long after the injury is inflicted. Forgiveness does not overlook what has happened, nor does it trivialize the injury by saying, "It's OKAY; its nothing, really." Forgiveness simply means that we no longer house "the bullet" and allow its poison to spread, in other words, we let God remove "the bullet." Of course, such "surgery" can be painful, but it is the first step toward healing.

Anyone who has recovered from an injury knows that healing is a gift, but one that requires hard work. For example, a woman who regained the use of an injured leg said that her healing process was both a miracle and a challenge. It was given to her, yet she had to work for it. No matter that the injury had been caused by someone else. To get well, she still had to follow the doctor's orders, and those orders included painful physical therapy. Miracle and challenge, gift and task—the description fits Jesus' words in Luke 17:3, 4 on forgiving others. These verses focus not on receiving forgiveness but on giving it.

First, Jesus says, "If another disciple sins, you must rebuke the offender" (17:3). Rebuke, strong reprimand, is the opposite of wimpy imitations of forgiveness in which people gloss over the hurt, murmuring that it's okay when it's not and never will be. Without a rebuke of some kind, the problem will not be named and offenses will continue to pile up. So Jesus tells us that we must speak plainly, not just suffer in silence. The rebuke gives the offender a moment of truth, a chance to change.

Second, Jesus says, "If there is repentance, you must forgive" (17:3). Repentance should come first—a person who has not repented can misuse forgiveness as a license for more sinning. Repentance is a way of turning around, of changing direction. If a person does repent, Jesus says that "you *must* forgive." He does not say that forgiving is an option to *consider*. Jesus sounds more like the surgeon who says, "That bullet has to come out." This is tough love, and its purpose is to make people well.

Now for the hard part. If this person sins against you seven times a day, yet "turns back to you seven times and says, 'I repent,' you must forgive," Jesus says. (17:4). Jesus calls his disciples to love one another in the same way God loves them. The disciples find this beyond their strength. They began to pray to the Lord, "Increase our faith" (v. 5). Most people find it difficult to forgive, especially when the injury is repeated. They prefer to carry the bullet inside. But in all difficulties and injuries, the Gospel heals. Those who do not yet forgive can at least begin to pray, "Lord, increase my faith." And God will do it.

Questions and Prayer

1. Have you received an "injury" that continues to do harm long after it was inflicted?

2. If there is such an injury in your life, what steps can be taken toward recovery?

3. Have you ever received a needed rebuke, or given one? What happened next?

Prayer: O God, you prescribe strong medicine for our injuries. Sometimes we would rather cherish the hurt than take the treatment. Show us your will and your way, O God, and make us whole in your powerful truth and grace. Amen.

FRIDAY

Read Luke 12:57-59. *"On the way make an effort to settle the case . . ."* (v. 58).

A GOOD COOK WHO grew up during the Great Depression had this motto: Use what you have. Perhaps a favorite recipe called for almonds and lemon, but almonds were too expensive and lemons were not always available. What to do? Revise the recipe or change the menu, but either way you have to eat! So use what you have. The same can be said of forgiveness.

Complete, full forgiveness calls for patience, trust, truth telling, repentance, confession, absolution, reconciliation, and change. Sometimes all the ingredients are on hand. Sometimes God provides the missing ingredients in answer to prayer.

But not always. One or more vital ingredients for forgiveness may be beyond reach and remain so. For example, suppose two people have hurt each other. One desires reconciliation, but the other party is no longer living. Or suppose that both people are living, but one wants to make amends and the other does not. Perhaps there is good reason to believe that repentance is lacking and further contact will only aggravate the injury. What to do? Follow the cook's advice and use the ingredients on hand. The ingredients include prayer, confession, and absolution, perhaps as part of a worship service or administered one-on-one by a pastor or trusted Christian friend.

Forgiveness takes many forms, all of which God uses to heal and bless. Author Gary Thomas, in an article titled "The Forgiveness Factor," describes varying degrees of forgiveness: (1) Detached forgiveness reduces negative feelings, although no reconciliation has taken place. (2) Limited forgiveness reduces negative feelings, restores a partial relationship, and decreases the emotional investment in the relationship. (3) Full forgiveness brings negative feelings to an end, and the restored relationship grows. Clearly, full forgiveness is the ideal, but even detached and limited forgiveness are better than none at all. Each is a gift from God. At the heart of any forgiveness is the "conscious decision not to seek revenge or nurse a grudge," but rather to forgive, Thomas writes. "This conversion of the heart is a critical stage toward forgiveness."

In one conversation with his disciples, Jesus spoke of "settling out of court." Here he intends something less than full forgiveness and reconciliation. There are times to cut one's losses and give up the idea of being 100 percent right. There are times to admit that the full ideal of forgiveness may not be realized in this life. There are even times to let go. Jesus advised that if someone has a grievance, try to settle "out of court," so to speak. Otherwise "you may be dragged before the judge, and the judge [will] hand you to an officer, and the officer [will] throw you into prison. I tell you, you will never get out until you have paid the very last penny" (12:58, 59). Sometimes a limited form of forgiveness can be better than insisting on complete resolution.

Jesus himself was no stranger to conflict; he would not compromise God's call even to save his own life. So when Jesus says that there are times to "settle out of court" he is not advising people to cave in to evil, sell out the truth, or gloss over injustice. His words simply imply that many of the conflicts we face and the injuries we suffer are not about matters of truth and justice. Not everything is of eternal consequence. In many instances, even partial forgiveness is better than carrying a pocket full of live coals. Total and complete forgiveness and reconciliation is a divine recipe. But if major ingredients are missing, God calls us to use what we have. Forgiveness may sometimes be partial, yet "the one who began a good work among you will bring it to completion by the day of Jesus Christ" (Phil. 1:6).

QUESTIONS AND PRAYER

1. Think of a time when you have experienced forgiveness from another person. Was this detached, limited, or full forgiveness?

2. Why is even detached or limited forgiveness better than none at all?

Prayer: Lord, you promised that the good work you have begun in us will be brought to completion on the day of Jesus Christ. Help us to use the ingredients of everyday life to forgive and receive forgiveness. We thank and praise you for this gift, and look forward to the day when your work will be complete in us. Amen.

SATURDAY

Read Luke 12:8-12. *"Everyone who speaks a word against the Son of Man will be forgiven; but whoever blasphemes against the Holy Spirit will not be forgiven"* (v. 10).

IT WAS SUNDAY IN MANHATTAN. A pastor and his family were walking up Broadway Avenue on their way home from church. The Gospel text for that day included Jesus' words on "the unforgivable sin," and the pastor had preached on that troubling theme. About twenty-five people had been present in the thread-bare church that day, and despite the prickly Gospel text and the pastor's earnest attempt to let that text speak, the service had seemed uneventful. Conversations after church were low-key. Walking home, the pastor wondered aloud if everyone had settled into the comfortable religion described by H. Richard Niebuhr, a religion in which "a God without wrath" brings people "without sin, into a kingdom without judgment, through the ministrations of a Christ without a cross." As the family walked home, talk soon drifted to options for dinner; "the unforgivable sin" seemed to have little to do with real life.

On the sidewalk ahead was a familiar figure: a gaunt-looking man with withered legs. His clothes were mismatched and he was unshaven. He sat in a wheelchair in front of a small run-down restaurant where the aroma of greasy chicken mixed with the diesel exhaust from the buses. The man was sitting in the same place every week when the pastor's family walked home from church; perhaps that spot was all he had to call home. The man had never spoken to the pastor before, but this time he stared intensely at the pastor's clergy shirt. As the family passed by, the man began to shout, "I cursed God today! I cursed God today!" It could have been a confession, but it sounded more like pure defiance. Was "the unforgivable sin," on which the pastor had just preached, being committed right then and there? The man's rage was a complete contrast to the bland worship service the family had just left.

Some people can be so complacent about God's love that they assume everything will be forgiven, without any repentance, confession, or desire for new life. Other people are certain their sins are too great for God to forgive; God's love, they think, will not stretch far enough to cover them.

In Luke 12:10, Jesus spoke of forgiveness with a promise for the fearful and a warning for the complacent. "Everyone who speaks a word against the Son of Man will be forgiven," he said, "but whoever blasphemes against the Holy Spirit will not be forgiven" (*to blaspheme* means "to revile, abuse, or speak of God with contempt"). This is not a feel-good verse, certainly, but it is an important one. It belongs in this journey through Lent with Luke. Jesus' promise and warning are for everyone.

The promise is that all sins "will be" forgiven, including the slander and contempt that people pour out upon Jesus. Even those who crucified him can be forgiven, as Jesus himself said from the cross: "Father, forgive them; for they do not know what they are doing" (23:34). Throughout the Gospel, Jesus teaches people to forgive, as God forgives them. A taste of resurrection, God's forgiveness conquers death and gives new life. The promise is generous, offered even to those who would crucify Christ.

But Jesus also issues a warning. There are people who, by their hard and impenitent hearts, are storing up divine wrath for themselves (Rom. 2:5). Those who treat God's forgiveness and the work of the Holy Spirit with contempt will not be forgiven. These days, when grace is such a pervasive theme, it is easy to neglect the warnings in Luke's Gospel (12:5, 20, 21, and many more). But they are there. Stern warnings jangle alongside promises and hope, like discordant notes in an otherwise lovely melody. Most people prefer to tune these notes out. But the point remains: God will not force grace upon those who consistently refuse it. If, on the last day, God says, "Have it your way, for all eternity," this will be a fearful judgment indeed.

The man on Broadway, shouting his curse at God, had reason to fear. God's judgment is not an empty threat. Jesus has warned that those who treat the Holy Spirit with contempt will be judged. But this same man also had reason to hope, because God's promise is not an empty one. God promises that all sins can be forgiven (Mark 3:28). Christ died under a rain of human curses, to bring God's mercy home. Therefore, heed the warning *and* cling to the promise. If the warning of judgment makes people uncomfortable, thanks be to God that the Spirit is at work.

Questions and Prayer

1. In what ways does God's grace change people?
2. What happens to the Christian faith when all warnings and consequences are taken away?

Prayer: Lord, you have promised that all sins "can be" forgiven, Move me to desire, seek, and cherish your gift of grace. Thank you for your great mercy. Amen.

Sunday

Read Luke 15:1-3, 11-32. *"There was a man who had two sons . . ."* (v. 11).

THE PARABLE IN LUKE 15, often called "The Story of the Prodigal Son," is the greatest forgiveness story of all. The are three characters: the runaway son, who repents; the son who stays at home, who resents; and the father, who loves both children.

This parable may inspire prayer, following a method known as T.R.I.P.© *T* stands for Thanksgiving, naming things in the parable that inspire thanks; *R* is for Regret, naming things that need to be confessed; *I* is for Intercession, bringing needs to God; and *P* is for Purpose, or Plan, seeking God's direction for living. This approach to praying with the scriptures draws insights from Martin Luther, and Walter and Ingrid Trobish.

Thanksgiving: Thank you, gracious God, for giving us freedom. The father in the parable allowed his young son to claim the inheritance, to make mistakes, and even to fail. Thank you for allowing us to take risks. Thank you for loving us, even when we run far away from you and end up hungry, penniless, and alone. Thank you for never giving up on us. You call us home and turn us around. Your Holy Spirit moves us to say, "I shall arise and go to my Father." Your mercy is great. You are waiting, watching, running to meet us along the road. You wrap us in mercy as in a rich robe. You set a feast before us. You welcome us home, again and again.

Regret: We confess, dear God, that we have often squandered your gifts and spurned your love. Some of us, like the younger son, have run far away from you and wasted your gifts. And some of us, like the older son, have lived "correctly," following all the rules, and have therefore felt deserving of more love, more blessings. We confess resenting your love toward others who seem less worthy than we consider ourselves. We repent that we are not satisfied simply to be with you. We confess that when you continue to love sinners, we don't want to celebrate. We repent for all the times we thought we would do a better job of being God than you do.

Intercession: Lord God, we pray for people who think they are beyond your calling range. We pray for those who run ever deeper into the night, lured by greed, addiction, hatred, unbelief, and despair. Where there is remorse, use it for healing. Where there is regret, use it for cleansing. Reach your beloved children and turn them toward home. Move all who are far from you to say, "I will arise and go to my Father!" May Jesus robe them in grace, and may the church welcome them with feasting and singing.

Dear God, we pray for all who live in your family the church, but who, like the older brother, brood on wrongs and will not let old bitterness depart. Create clean hearts and renew right spirits within us all. Show us that in your sight we are all alike.

Purpose: Lord, as you forgive us, move us to forgive others. Make us faithful in prayer for people in our lives who seem to have wandered far from you and for people who have hurt us. May we rejoice and give thanks for each new child of God, for each person who turns toward you. As the returning son wore the father's robe and ring and shoes, may we wear your mercy, cling to your promises, and claim your Word as our inheritance forever. Amen.

QUESTION AND PRAYER

1. Where do you see yourself in the parable of the prodigal son?

Prayer: For today's prayer, try using the T.R.I.P.© meditation above.

WEEK 5: BELIEVING 🔥

J ESUS CALLS CHRISTIANS TO FAITH. In his teachings and by his
example, he showed the power of believing in God. He also
gave the disciples—continues to give Christians—new opportunities for believing

MONDAY

Read Luke 5:1-11. *"Master, we have worked all night long but have caught
nothing. Yet if you say so, I will let down the nets"* (v. 5).

"THERE MUST NOT BE ANY FISH IN THIS LAKE," a brother said to
his sister as they brought in their hooks and lines. Up since dawn,
they'd rented a boat and made their way across the lake to a
secluded point fringed by rushes and lily pads. There they tried
different baits and even different fishing spots, but not a single fish
bit on their lines. "They're not biting today," said the sister.
"Maybe the weather's been too hot." "No," said the brother, "there
just aren't any fish in this lake." Finally they gave up and headed
back to the dock. Trudging toward their van, they glanced over at
the fish-cleaning house just beyond the parking lot. Through the
screened windows they could see two men scaling fish. Walking
over for a closer look, the brother and sister were astonished to see
that these wily old fishermen had two stringers of bass and large
sunfish, enough for a hearty fish fry. "Didn't you say that there
were no fish in this lake?" said the sister. "Well," replied the
brother, "maybe those fish were caught somewhere else!"

It takes faith to go fishing. You have to believe that there are fish in the lake and that the fish might bite. Several of Jesus' disciples were fishermen, and Jesus promoted them to fish for people. It all started one day when Jesus was teaching crowds of people on the shores of Galilee. To better address the crowds, Jesus got into one of the boats and asked Simon to put out a little from shore. When he had finished speaking to the people, he asked Simon to put out into deep water and let down the nets for a catch. Simon's reply may have been weary, "We worked all night long"; discouraged, "We caught nothing"; or skeptical, "If you say so." But Simon did as Jesus said and let down the nets. Soon there were so many fish that the nets were breaking. Simon signaled the men in the other boat to help. Both boats became so laden with fish that they were about to sink. It seemed like a practical joke, a divine comedy of flopping fish, sloshing water, tearing nets, and astonished fishermen.

Just a moment before the great catch, Peter had every reason to doubt that one more try would make any difference. But Jesus did not ask if Peter was ready or in the mood to believe. He simply gave Peter a moment for believing—not abstract believing, as when one "believes" that a cloud floating by is real, but active believing, as when one pulls on the oars and then lets wet nets slip through rough hands into dark waters one more time. Such active believing starts with God's call: "Lord, *if you say so.*" Peter sensed God's presence and cried, "Depart from me, Lord, for I am a sinful man." But Jesus answered, "Do not be afraid; from now on you will be catching people" (5:10).

God keeps calling people to believe in Jesus and follow him. The call comes to those who are hopeful, of course, but it also comes to those who are discouraged. God's call comes even to those who suspect that there are no fish in the lake, who think

71

that God will never use them, who fear that nothing can ever change. God has a way of asking us to try one more time even after we have already given up. It is God's persistent call that persuades us, sometimes in spite of ourselves, to "let down the nets for a catch." "Lord, if you say so!"

Questions and Prayer

1. In the story of the great fish harvest, why didn't Jesus just have the fish jump into the boat, without any effort on the part of the fishermen?

2. Is there a discouraging situation or relationship in which God might be asking you to try one more time?

3. When and where does God's call come to us? Is it necessary for people to be in the right frame of mind before God calls?

Prayer: Lord, sometimes we get discouraged when the fish just aren't biting. Thank you for calling us in spite of ourselves. Help us to tell others about Jesus. Amen.

Tuesday

Read Luke 8:4-8, 11-15. *"The seed is the word of God"* (v. 11).

WHY DO SOME PEOPLE BELIEVE and others do not? The mystery of faith and unbelief has troubled Christians through the centuries. Jesus' parable of the sower explores this mystery.

Planted in human life, God's call is a seed from which faith grows. According to Jesus, however, there are some people with the soil of their hearts so hardened that God's word does not sink in. As in a field where birds swoop down to devour every seed that falls, God's word can be snatched away by distractions, fears, and excuses before it can germinate. Some seeds fall on shallow, rocky ground, where there is not much soil. These seeds spring up quickly, but the sun beats down and scorches the seedlings. Lacking any depth of soil, these seedlings wither away. Some people receive God's word gladly, but their shallow faith cannot survive the heat.

Still other seeds fall among thorns that grow up and choke them. Many people hear God's word, but worldly cares and delight in riches constrict it so it cannot thrive. Jesus says that both cares and riches can choke his Word. When life is too hard, or too easy, faith may wither. If a garden is overrun by weeds, it matters little if the weeds have thorns or flowers, or some of each, like a thistle. The weeds take the best sunlight, water, and soil so that the tomatoes and green beans languish. So it is in human life. The Gospel is by no means the only plant in life's garden.

Yet, Jesus says, some seed falls on good soil. People who hear the word, those who "hold it fast in an honest and good heart, and bear fruit with patient endurance"(8:15), are good soil. In their lives the seed produces. Jesus wants God's word to take root, grow strong, and produce a harvest of faith.

Faith and unbelief are a mystery, but an even greater wonder is God's lavish grace. No one knows why God sows the word with such reckless abandon, throwing it into the most unlikely places. In the parable, the sower is "broadcasting," an ancient method of planting in which seeds are cast broadly by the handful, falling on soil, stones, and pathways. What a contrast with methods of planting in which only fertile soil, carefully prepared, receives the seed!

Today the word *broadcasting* is used to describe the transmitting of messages through mass media. There is no telling who might "tune in." In the same way, there is no telling who might hear the Gospel and believe it. God does not seem to calculate just where the seed has the best chance to grow. Instead God is lavish with the word and does not hold back. To be sure, many things can prevent the seed from growing. Despite its size, however, this seed is tough and resilient. The wonder is, how much of it does grow and thrive.

God's word changes hearts and lives, just as a seed can change the soil; indeed, plants can change an entire landscape. So, too, God's word can change human lives and communities.

Instead of planting the Word selectively among just the "right" people, God is in the business of broadcasting.

Questions and Prayer

1. In your own life's garden, what competes with God's word?

2. Why do you think God "broadcasts" the Gospel instead of planting it carefully in places where it is sure to grow?

Prayer: O God, you plant your word so generously, even in places where it seems to have little chance to grow. Thank you for being so generous. Help us to receive your word with joy, and in turn to plant it freely all around us. Amen.

Wednesday

Read Luke 8:22-25. *"While they were sailing, he fell asleep"* (v. 23).

Saganaga Lake, which borders the United States and Canada, was well named. *Saganaga* means "lake that bewilders." With its many islands and bays, Saganaga still bewilders even travelers who are good at reading maps. Saganaga has big open waters too, smooth as glass on a rare calm day, but whipped to a white froth on a windy day. No one would choose to be out on "Big Sag" when the white caps are rolling, but sometimes the wind catches people off guard.

One day three friends set out in their canoe across Saganaga. One paddled in the bow, one in the stern, and the third, the "duffer," rode in the middle. As the three friends pushed off from shore, the water looked a bit choppy. When they reached open water, they could see white caps in the distance. As the wind shoved the water into waves, the two paddlers tried to keep the bow pointed straight into the wind as the waves began to roll higher. With great effort, the paddlers steered the bow to pierce each crest, making the small craft ride up and smack down on each wave—a hard ride but safer than being swamped from the side. Even so, the canoe was taking on water. Muscles ached and blisters rose as the paddlers kept straining for the distant shore. The trees seemed to cower beneath the darkening sky as thunder rolled in from the west.

Meanwhile, the duffer was no help at all. Sitting in the bilge water at the bottom of the canoe, his head resting on a packsack, he slept. "How can he sleep at such a time?" the paddlers wondered. "He should wake up and bail water out of the canoe, encourage us to keep going, and pray that God will keep the canoe from capsizing in the freezing lake. And to think that this whole trip was *his* idea in the first place!" Yes, it was he, the duffer, who said, "Let's go across to the other side of the lake."

Through the stinging spray, the duffer heard, "Master, Master, we are perishing!" (8:24). That's right, the duffer is Jesus.

Now awake, Jesus feels the wild wind, he feels the icy spray at the bow, he sees the dark clouds and the churning waves. He lifts his face to water and sky. He says to the wind, "Turn back," and to the sea, "Peace, be still." The wind stops. The waves subside. There is a flat calm. "Where is your faith?" Jesus asks. Amazed, yet afraid, the paddlers marvel, "Who is this, that even the winds and the waves obey him?" (8:25). Jesus has calmed the storm.

Some Christians find it extremely difficult to trust Jesus in a storm. Thank God, Jesus does not require perfect faith or calculate how strongly people believe before he will save us. Yet Jesus wants every disciple to grow in faith and become stronger in believing. Though he sometimes seems to be sleeping, Jesus hears all questions. He hears *our* questions: "Wake up, Lord! Don't you care if we perish?" And Jesus also questions *us:* "Where is your faith?" God's power to save is greater than the wind and the waves. In this story, Jesus' friends naturally want him to use that power on their behalf, especially when they are in trouble. Yet even when Jesus is not doing what his friends want him to do, it is enough just to be with him, in the same boat.

QUESTIONS AND PRAYER

1. Who is Jesus, that even the winds and the waves obey him?
2. How do we know Jesus is with us, even when he does not seem to be helping us?

❧

Prayer: O God, you are with us on the stormy sea of life. Thank you for calming the storms. Thank you for being with us. Thank you for giving us faith. Amen.

THURSDAY

Read Luke 9:18-20. *"But who do you say that I am?"* (v. 20).

ONCE WHEN JESUS AND THE DISCIPLES were alone, away from the crowds, Jesus asked them, "Who do the people say that I am?" The disciples replied, "Some people think you are John the Baptist come back to life." (John, who preached repentance and baptism for the forgiveness of sins, had been executed in prison under Herod.) "And others think that you are Elijah." (God had promised, in Malachi 4:5, to send the prophet Elijah to "turn the hearts of parents to their children and the hearts of children to their parents" so that God would not come and strike the land with a curse.) "Still others," the disciples continued, "say that you are another one of the ancient prophets." (The prophets were God's messengers, chosen to convict people of sin and also to bring hope. Indeed, Jesus began his public ministry by reading from the prophet Isaiah, proclaiming good news to the poor and release to the captives. Luke 4:8 shows that like other prophets, Jesus was rejected by his own friends and neighbors.) Each answer had a glimmer of truth. These notions about Jesus were not wrong; they were just too small.

Today people have many different ideas about who Jesus is. Some honor Jesus as the founder of a world religion, on par with Moses, Muhammad, or Buddha. Others see Jesus as a great teacher whose sayings, prayers, and parables still speak to us today. Others call him a healer. Still others say he was a prophet, afflicting the comfortable and comforting the afflicted. Each of these answers also has a glimmer of truth. Yet none of them, or even all of them taken together, fully tells us who Jesus is. The "founder" or "teacher" or "healer" or "prophet" speaks only of who Jesus *was*, not who he *is*, let alone who Jesus is *to us*.

After the disciples told Jesus what the crowds were saying about him, Jesus turned and asked them, "Who do *you* say that I am?" Jesus still asks this question every day. It is a question that invites faith. Not content just to hear what other people say about him, Jesus asks who he is to *us*.

When Jesus asked, "Who do you do you say that I am?" Peter answered, "The Messiah of God." Jesus warned the disciples not to tell anyone that he was the Messiah until his work was complete. First he must suffer, die, and rise from the dead. Now that his work is accomplished, Christians are witnesses to it.

Believing in Jesus as living Lord and Savior means answering the question "Who do you say that I am?" with words and with lives, every day. The apostle Paul wrote, "The word is near you, on your lips and in your heart . . . because if you confess with your lips that Jesus is Lord and believe in your heart that God raised him from the dead, you will be saved" (Rom. 10:8-9). Believing in Jesus cannot be contained inside the believer. Faith flows out in words and deeds, just as water rushes from a fountain. Believing rises up to greet Jesus' question, "Who do you say that I am?"

Questions and Prayer

1. Who do people you know say that Jesus is?

2. Who do you say that Jesus is?

Prayer: Lord God, your Word is near us, on our lips and in our hearts. You have promised that if we confess with our lips that Jesus is Lord and believe in our hearts that God raised him from the dead, we will be saved. Give us grace to make this confession and believe it today and always. Amen.

Friday

Read Luke 9:21-25. *"For those who want to save their life will lose it, and those who lose their life for my sake will save it"* (v. 24).

Over a huge waterfall there stretched a tightrope. Eager spectators clustered around two small wooden platforms, one on each side of the falls. From a platform at one end of the tightrope, an acrobat called to his audience, "Do you believe that I can cross the falls by walking on a tightrope?" Some were skeptical, others thought it could be done. A few spectators cried out, "Yes, go ahead. Let's see if you can." Armed with nothing but his pole for balance, the acrobat stepped out on the high wire, the great chasm of thundering spray looming below.

Carefully he made his way across and stepped from the wire onto the opposite platform. The crowd whistled and cheered. Then he asked them, "Do you believe that I can push a wheelbarrow across the tightrope to the other side?" This time, many were optimistic. They'd seen him cross once and believed he could do it again. Most of them called out, "Yes, yes, you can do it!" The acrobat took his wheelbarrow, positioned it with great care, and stepped out onto the tightrope once again. Slowly he made his way out over the falls, placing just enough weight forward onto the wheelbarrow to maintain perfect balance. Crossing above the roaring waters, he made his way to the platform where he had first begun. This time the crowd shouted and whistled like true believers. All traces of skepticism were gone.

The acrobat rested for a few moments, mopping his brow with a handkerchief and refreshing himself with a drink of water. Then he addressed the crowd: "Now do you believe that I can push this wheelbarrow across the waterfall?" Having just seen him do this, they cheered with gusto. "Do you believe that I can take a passenger across the falls in this wheelbarrow?" he asked. Once more the people cheered wildly. This was getting to be quite a show. "Very well, then," he said. "Who would like to get in?"

Jesus asks us, "Who do you say that I am?" Christians confess that Jesus is the Son of God, who died, rose, and is coming again. This belief is very important, yet faith is more than this. Believing means that, because of who Jesus is and what he has done, his followers actually "get in." It means that we put our lives in his hands. Jesus can be trusted to carry us across life and death. On the other hand, those who do not entrust their lives to Jesus will never find true life. Jesus said that people who want to save their lives will instead lose their lives, and those who lose their lives for his sake will be saved (9:24).

Jesus said, "If any want to become my followers, let them deny themselves and take up their cross daily and follow me" (9:23). To believe in Jesus is to follow him, taking up a cross. Christians sometimes speak of "cross bearing" because God may allow suffering for a purpose. This can help people trust Jesus through difficult times. But notice that Jesus said, "Those who lose their life *for my sake* will save it." Not every "cross" in life is from God. Suffering for his sake means suffering because one believes, loves, and serves Jesus. Such suffering is redemptive; it can be used by the Holy Spirit to help and save others. These are times to trust Jesus to carry us across a chasm.

Believing in Jesus means following him, and sometimes being carried by him, through life and death. As the tightrope walker who crossed the waterfall knew, there's a great deal of difference between the person who cheers from the sidelines and the person who will get into the wheelbarrow.

QUESTIONS AND PRAYER

1. How does the story of the tightrope walker illustrate faith?

2. Can you think of a time when suffering (your own or someone else's) has been used to help, or save, others?

3. When have you been carried by Jesus?

Prayer: O Jesus, you said that those who lose their lives for your sake will save them, and that those who suffer for your sake are blessed. Lead us every day so that we may fulfill your purpose for us and help us to trust you. Amen.

SATURDAY

Read Luke 8:48; 17:19; 18:42. *"Your faith has made you well"* (17:19).

ONCE THERE WAS A DEVOUT CHRISTIAN MAN who had lung cancer and who believed that God would cure him if he had enough faith. He drew inspiration from many places in the Bible where faith and healing are linked, such as the stories of the woman who was healed of a flow of blood (8:48), the man cleansed of leprosy (17:19), and the blind man who received his sight (18:42). The devout Christian man had experienced healing before and had great faith in God, yet this time his cancer had gotten worse. He began to blame himself, thinking that he was not cured because his life was not pleasing to God or because he did not have enough faith. Thus, in the weeks before his death, he was deprived of the comfort faith could have given him, just when he needed it most. This man was right to believe that God has the power to heal, and he was right to look to Scripture for guidance. But his belief that faith *always* results in the cure of a disease was misguided. Even Lazarus, whom Jesus raised from the dead, would one day die again. The only permanent cure for mortality is resurrection.

To be sure, there are moments in the Gospel when faith seems to precipitate healing, just as thunder ushers in a rainstorm. When the woman in search of healing dares to touch Jesus' garment, she is healed. When the blind man shouts for Jesus' attention, despite being shushed by the crowd, he receives his sight. But there are also moments when healing seems to come without faith; for example, of the ten lepers Jesus cleansed, only one, a Samaritan, came back to thank him. For this particular Samaritan, it was only *after* the healing, and *after* he had returned to thank Jesus, that he heard Jesus say, "Your faith has made you well." For this Samaritan, now healed of leprosy, complete healing involved praising and thanking God. Physical healing was a significant part of this man's experience, but his attitude of gratitude seems to have been even more important to Jesus.

The relationship between faith and healing is deep, yet elusive. It is not like adding two and two to get four. Indeed, the New Testament includes a great variety of combinations of faith and healing. There is faith before healing, as in the stories from Luke noted above. There is faith after healing (see the story of the man born blind in John 9). There is faith with no healing (in John 11, Lazarus is allowed to die, despite his family's strong devotion to Jesus). As in the Bible, so today each human story is unique.

There is more to healing than the cure of an ailment. It is possible to be cured but not healed, for whoever has health without faith is still out of joint with God. Believing in Jesus is the most important thing, whether or not there is physical healing. It is possible to rejoice in God's promises even when one suffers: "Though our outer nature is wasting away, our inner nature is being renewed every day." Things suffered in this life prepare Christians for "an eternal weight of glory, beyond all comparison, because we look not to the things that are seen but to the things that are unseen" (2 Cor. 4:16-18). Unbelief is the greatest disease, and the greatest healing is faith.

Questions and Prayer

1. What could you say to someone who says, "God would heal me if only I had enough faith"?

2. Does the statement "the greatest disease is unbelief" ring true for you? Why or why not?

Prayer: O God, creator of all life, you have the power to heal those who are sick, and you are always at work healing. Help us to place our confidence in you, not in how much or how little faith we ourselves may have. Amen.

SUNDAY

Read Luke 17:5-6. *"If you had faith the size of a mustard seed . . ."* (v. 6).

MEASURING SPOONS AND CUPS help cooks to add just the right amount of salt, baking soda, or sugar to make a recipe come out right. If the ingredients are out of proportion, the bread will not rise, the stew will be too salty, or the pancake batter will be too thin. People sometimes think of faith as though it were an ingredient to be measured like sugar or salt. "If only I had a little more faith," people say, "I might be healed." Or, "She sure has a lot of faith. . . . I wish I had that much faith."

To be sure, there are people whose lives shine with a vibrant faith, and others in whom faith seems to flicker like a candle flame about to drown in its own wax. But how much faith is enough? After Jesus told the disciples that they must keep on forgiving one who repents, the disciples asked him to increase their faith (17:5), as if to say, "Lord, if you are going to give us such hard work, raise our pay!" At that point, Jesus could have prescribed a faith-building exercise program, guaranteed to strengthen faith. Instead Jesus said something strange: "If you had faith the size of a mustard seed, you could say to this mulberry tree, 'Be uprooted and planted in the sea,' and it would obey you" (v. 6). In other words, even the tiniest speck of faith is enough. Believing and following Jesus does not require a certain *quantity* of faith. Rather, Jesus wants each person to use the faith he has already given, even if it is only a speck.

If someone keeps a large jar of yeast in the refrigerator but never uses it, this quantity of yeast will never raise a batch of dough. Yet even a small amount, if used, mixed with warm water and flour, can make a whole loaf rise. Jesus said that the kingdom of God is like "yeast that a woman took and mixed in with three measures of flour, until all of it was leavened" (13:21). Jesus named a quantity for flour, but not for yeast. The amount of yeast is not as important as is the putting it to work in the dough.

Many people have packets of garden seeds that never get planted. No matter how many seeds there are, those seeds will not grow while they stay in the envelope. The act of planting is more important than having a large quantity in stock. Jesus compared the kingdom of God to "a mustard seed that someone took and sowed in the garden. It grew and became a tree, and the birds of the air made nests in its branches" (13:19). God can use even a small speck of faith to shelter and feed others.

Faith cannot be measured, nor can it be kept in a closed container and stored up for some future use. In Old Testament times, when God's people wandered in the wilderness, they were fed on manna, a special food sent by God. Each day God fed them just enough. Some people tried to gather a larger supply so that they could feel more secure about tomorrow, but when they did so, the manna spoiled (Exod. 16:19-20). God wanted them to live by faith, using the manna God provided day by day.

So it is with believing. Faith is meant to be planted, mixed, invested, and reinvested every day. Rather than measure or even protect faith, Jesus calls us to let faith work and breathe and live.

Faith is meant to be used. The disciples prayed, "Lord, increase our faith." Jesus wanted them to use what he gave, even if it was just a tiny speck.

QUESTIONS AND PRAYER

1. Have you ever said (or heard someone say), "I'd like to do this or that, but I just don't have enough faith"? How much faith is enough?

2. Name one situation in your life where you could put even a little speck of faith to work.

Prayer: Holy Spirit, faith comes from you as a gift. We thank and praise you for giving us faith, even if it seems like just a little bit. Help us use the faith you give us. Amen.

WEEK 6: DARING

A S THE SEASON OF LENT DRAWS CLOSER TO HOLY WEEK, this journey with Luke through Lent meets daring and confrontation. "Lite" versions of Christianity want to make everyone comfortable. But Jesus' life was full of conflict: strife with the religious leaders of his day, wrangles among his disciples, assaults from Satan the tempter, confrontations with death. This rocky pathway led him to the cross.

MONDAY

Read Luke 4:24-30. "No prophet is accepted in the prophet's hometown" (v. 24).

SOON AFTER JESUS WAS BAPTIZED, he was tempted by the devil for forty days in the wilderness (4:2). Rejecting Satan's empty promises and daring to remain faithful to God, Jesus returned to Galilee "filled with the power of the Spirit" (v. 14). Since Jesus had grown up in Galilee, everyone praised and admired him as he taught in the local synagogues there.

When Jesus came to his hometown of Nazareth, where people had known him since childhood, he stood in the synagogue and read from the prophet Isaiah: "The Spirit of the Lord is upon me, because he has anointed me to bring good news to the poor. He has sent me to proclaim release to the captives and recovery of sight to the blind, to let the oppressed go free, to proclaim the year of the Lord's favor" (4:18-19). Rolling up the scroll, Jesus proclaimed, "Today this scripture has been fulfilled in your hearing" (4:21). The crowd was pleased and everyone spoke well of him, as people do today when they say, "Nice sermon, pastor."

But Jesus knew that approval is not the same thing as faith. He might as well have preached to these hometown folk in an unknown language. Some people were saying, "Isn't this Joseph's son?" as though they wanted to cut this bold Jesus down to a manageable size. God had appeared in person proclaiming the kingdom, and the people felt good because their hometown boy was famous. Perhaps now he could do a few favors for them, since, after all, they knew him when he was little. If Jesus had made them comfortable, he could have been popular indeed. But he pressed on with God's message: "The Spirit of the Lord is upon me."

Jesus now cut through hometown sentiment with the edge of Scripture. "What about that time," Jesus asked them, "when there was a famine and God sent Elijah to help a foreign widow rather than helping those at home?" He persisted, "What about that time when God chose to cleanse a Syrian leper and left the hometown folks unhealed?" They were hometown folks, but God owed them no favors. With God, there are no insiders and outsiders. There is only faith and unbelief.

These sharp words laid bare the core of unbelief in every heart. What a dangerous thing for Jesus to do! Jesus had spoiled the crowd's good feeling and their mood turned ugly. Like a flooding river that sweeps away all before it, the angry townspeople surged around Jesus. They pushed him out of town and rushed him out to a high place, where they intended to hurl him over the edge. There stood Jesus, a cliff behind him and a mob in front of him. Then, like a man wading through a flood, Jesus walked through the middle of the crowd. As he went on his way, no one dared to touch him.

Questions and Prayer

1. Jesus said, "The Spirit of the Lord is upon me." How do Jesus' actions (in Luke 4:24-30, or in general) show the presence of the Holy Spirit?

2. What did the townsfolk expect of Jesus?

3. Why didn't Jesus conform to these expectations?

Prayer: Jesus, you will not be made captive to our limited view of you. Thank you for challenging us. Help us to know, love, and serve you better. Amen.

Tuesday

Read Luke 5:29-32. *"Why do you eat and drink with tax collectors and sinners?"* (v. 30).

MOST ADULTS CAN REMEMBER PLAYING BASEBALL during recess or gym class. The gym teacher would select two captains and then the captains would choose teams, usually by picking the best players first. The fast runners, strong hitters, and good throwers and catchers would be chosen first, leaving the slow and awkward kids standing there unchosen. How hard it is to be among the last ones picked, and then to hear the elite, first-chosen players say, "Oh no, not *her!*" or, "Do we have to have *him?*" Perhaps by now people have found more humane ways to form teams. Still, life holds many other occasions when people are chosen or not chosen, even in the church.

When Jesus chose his team of disciples, the stakes were very high. The disciples would be key players in the Gospel story, and it was important to pick winners. If Jesus had consulted professional leaders, they might well have advised him: "First, choose people with good reputations. That way, you avoid public relations problems and easily win the trust of ordinary people for the new movement. Second, choose people with expertise in religion. This deflects criticism from professionals and saves the trouble of having to teach your disciples everything from scratch. Third, choose people who are well connected to money and political power, which always come in handy."

Jesus could have built the right kind of team by following these guidelines. But he did not choose the people with the best reputation, training, or connections. He dared to choose ordinary people. Some were just plain unqualified, and others (from the Pharisees' points of view) were downright liabilities. Take, for example, Levi the tax collector. Tax collectors, as already noted, were often hated. Levi was sitting at his toll booth when Jesus called, "Follow me." Levi got up, left everything behind, and followed Jesus. Levi was so happy that he gave a great banquet for Jesus and invited many other "tax collectors and sinners." There sat Jesus, eating with these ne'er-do-wells, heedless of his reputation. Calling Levi had been no passing whim or blunder. Jesus was daring to associate with all the "wrong" people. As if one tax collector were not enough of a public relations problem, Jesus allowed himself to be seen with a whole crowd of them. Surely, thought the Pharisees, Jesus must realize that people judge him by the company he keeps. So these religious leaders grumbled, "Why do you eat and drink with tax collectors and sinners?"

Jesus replied, "Those who are well have no need of a physician but those who are sick. I have come not to call the righteous, but sinners to repentance" (5:31, 32). Instead of choosing the team that could best help him to succeed, Jesus chose the people who needed him most, those who had no reason to expect to be chosen. Time after time, Jesus' actions offended the religious professionals, and as a result many of these leaders became his enemies.

Yet offending the professionals, daring as it was, was not what moved Jesus to choose his unlikely bunch of disciples. Jesus acted from faith in God's power to save sinners. Jesus' call changes people, setting them on a new path in life. To Levi the tax collector, Jesus did not say, "I affirm you. Stay right where you are and continue leading the life you have come to know." Instead he said, "Follow me." Nor did Jesus say, "I have come to tell sinners to remain as they are." Instead he called sinners to repentance. *Repentance* means "turning around, starting over, leaving the past behind." Jesus does not call disciples for their attainments, skills, or reputations; Jesus calls people for what God wants to make of them. When it comes to choosing and making disciples, no one can equal Jesus for sheer daring.

Questions and Prayer

1. How does your congregation, employer, or community choose people to be on "teams"?

2. Whom does Jesus choose to follow him?

3. What makes Jesus' statement "I have come not to call the righteous but sinners to repentance" (5:32) the heart of the Gospel?

Prayer: Lord Jesus, your call changes people. You call us to repentance, turning us from old ways so that we may follow you. Give us courage to answer your call day by day. Amen.

Wednesday

Read Luke 16:1-9. *"And his master commended the dishonest manager because he had acted shrewdly"* (v. 8).

POPULAR WISDOM SAYS THAT there are three kinds of people: those who make things happen, those who watch things happen, and those who wonder what happened. Jesus told a parable about someone who made things happen. This man is a manager, or steward, in charge of his master's estate. Accused of squandering the master's property, the man is about to be fired. Just a few hours remain before he will have to turn in his laptop and surrender his office keys and business cards. No more company logo and letterhead; good-bye to phone, fax, and support staff.

Time is running out, so the man does a personal inventory of his skills. He concludes that he is "not strong enough to dig, and ashamed to beg" (16:3). He decides to do some quick favors for people so that they will help him when he's out of a job. With nothing to offer but his boss's wealth and good name, he goes to people who are in debt to the master. As they look over his shoulder, he changes the accounts and reduces their debts—as the saying goes, "When all else fails, manipulate the data"— hoping that later these people will remember what he did for them if and when he needs to call in a favor.

When the manager goes to present accounts to his master, one would naturally expect the master to tell him that he's been caught doctoring the accounts and rebuke his dishonest employee. But that's not the way Jesus tells it. Jesus says that the master commends the dishonest manager. *To commend* is "to praise, affirm, appreciate, or approve." The master commends the manager for acting shrewdly, "for the children of this age are more shrewd in dealing with their own generation than are the children of light" (16:8). This manager makes things happen; he does not just sit back and watch things happen or wonder what happened!

God knows, people can be quite resourceful and shrewd in looking out for themselves. What if Christians were equally savvy in looking out for God's interests? What if Christians, in serving God, were as bold, clever, and quick as all the other folks who are out there hustling?

Jesus' parable is as sly as a barbed fishhook. People have spent a lot of time trying to straighten out this story by arguing that the manager was really okay after all. Some find it just plain irritating that this dishonest manager is held up as an example. Could not Jesus have chosen someone more praiseworthy for his followers to emulate? While his hearers are still wondering what happened, Jesus sets the hook: "And I tell you, make friends for yourselves by means of dishonest wealth, so that when it is gone, they may welcome you into the eternal homes" (16:9).

In other words, dare to use earthly things for heavenly ends. Use the things that *don't* last (money, skills, and influence) for the sake of things that *do* (eternal life, God's kingdom, God's love). The steward was daring because he knew that he had only a short time left in his stewardship. So, too, for us: Time is short. Christians do not own the Gospel but are temporary stewards of it. Jesus wants Christians to serve him with as much savvy and energy as do "the children of this age" (16:8).

God's people often operate slowly and timidly, as though our own resources are all we have to work with. Jesus' parable, in contrast, dares Christians to operate out of abundance—not our own abundance but God's. Rather than watch things happen or wonder what happened, Christians can make things happen when, like the manager in the parable, we dare to draw on God's account and use the Master's good name.

Questions and Prayer

1. Are we as quick to serve the Lord as we are to serve our own interests?

2. What can be learned from the example of the dishonest manager in Jesus' story?

Prayer: Gracious God, you are generous in mercy and you bless us abundantly. Help us to use your good name and share your gifts with others, and make us bold and resourceful stewards. Amen.

Thursday

Read Luke 9:1-6. *"And he sent them out to proclaim the kingdom of God and to heal"* (v. 2).

"What was your first solo flight like?" a student pilot was asked. "It was frightening," the young pilot admitted, "and thrilling too! I had to take everything my flight instructor said and make it my own. I was alone in the cockpit, yet I felt very close to my teacher. Best of all, the view was great!"

Jesus' disciples also had a solo flight, but theirs was in ministry. Before they tried their wings, Jesus "gave them power and authority over all demons and to cure diseases, and he sent them out to proclaim the kingdom of God and to heal" (9:1-2). Soon Jesus sent out seventy more people to proclaim the kingdom (10:1-12). After Easter, Jesus promised his followers, "You will receive power when the Holy Spirit has come upon you; and you will be my witnesses in Jerusalem, in all Judea and Samaria, and to the ends of the earth" (Acts 1:8). It takes daring to obey such a commission, and Jesus asks each Christian to dare. Christians can listen for Jesus' call using the T.R.I.P.© guide to prayer with Luke 9:1-6, the story of the disciples' first solo flight.

Thanksgiving: Thank you, Lord, for calling and entrusting ordinary people with your Gospel. Thank you for using everyday people to proclaim Christ to the world and to heal. Thank you, Lord, for giving your own power and authority to those whom you call and send. Thank you for giving faith, courage, and obedience to your people. Thank you for sending messengers of your kingdom all over the world. Thank you for the grace, hope, and healing that comes from your Gospel.

Regret: Lord, you told the disciples, "Take nothing for your journey, no staff, nor bag, nor bread, nor even an extra tunic" (9:3). You have allowed us much more carry-on baggage than those first disciples could have imagined, yet we are never satisfied. We repent that our love of comfort, security, and possessions sometimes keeps us from serving and following you. You told the disciples, "Whatever house you enter, stay there, and leave from there" (9:5). Forgive the times we have taken hospitality for granted, the times we have looked elsewhere for a better deal.

Forgive us for compromising your message, at times beyond recognition. You told the disciples that they would not always be welcomed, yet we expect to be liked and appreciated. We repent of expecting better treatment than you yourself received.

Intercession. We pray, dear Lord, for your servants who leave home, family, and possessions to follow you. Help and strengthen Christians who suffer for your name's sake, especially those in prison or in danger. We pray for missionaries and pastors around the world, that they may proclaim Christ faithfully. Bless people who offer hospitality to your servants: May they receive abundantly from your treasure store of faith, hope, and love. Bless seminary and college students, and all who prepare for lives of service. Bring them through uncertain times, prosper their studies, and guide them in their vocations. Strengthen doctors and nurses, teachers and social workers, and all who practice healing and mercy. Help parents to care for the children you entrust to them. Give to each of your children the courage to discern and follow your call.

Purpose. Lord Jesus, you give your disciples a purpose: to serve and follow you. You promise to be with us all the way. Help us to hear your voice. Dare us to travel lighter, so that nothing prevents us from following you. Free our hearts and minds to serve you. We are never ready for your call, yet you call us today. May we hear and answer you. Amen.

Question and Prayer

1. What hinders you from serving Christ?

Prayer: For today's prayer, use the T.R.I.P.© devotion above.

Friday

Read Luke 9:57-62. *"I will follow you wherever you go"* (v. 57).

In "virtual reality," part of the electronic age, people see images, play games, and even go on trips on their computer screens. It all seems very real, but it isn't. Luke 9:57-62 tells of Jesus' encounter with three "virtual," or would-be, disciples who want to follow him—but only if their lives could remain unchanged.

As Jesus and his disciples were walking along the road, the first would-be follower said to him, "I will follow you wherever you go." Jesus could have replied, "That's great, come along with us and we will do everything we can to make you comfortable." But instead Jesus said, "Foxes have holes, and birds of the air have nests, but the Son of Man has nowhere to lay his head" (9:58).

Following Jesus took faith then, as it does now. People who like to know what to expect—those who prefer pre-planned itineraries, hotel reservations, and climate control—will find that following Jesus is more than they bargained for. To be sure, Jesus and his disciples sometimes made "reservations" ahead of time (9:52; 22:11), but usually there was no confirmed campsite, let alone a permanent address. Jesus said that wild animals like foxes and birds had more security. Luke does not say that the first inquirer followed Jesus; most likely he remained a "virtual disciple."

To a second would-be disciple Jesus said, "Follow me." This one replied, "Lord, first let me go and bury my father." Most people will excuse family members from almost any task so that they can attend a funeral. Thus, Jesus might be expected to have said, "Go and bury your father, and then return to me." But instead Jesus responded, "Let the dead bury their own dead; but as for you, go and proclaim the kingdom of God" (9:60).

Although surprisingly harsh, these words are also full of promise. Jesus frees people from death's dominion. Grief and mourning are part of life, but Jesus makes a stronger claim. The statement "Let the dead bury their own dead" dares people to belong to the *living* Christ. "As for you," said Jesus, "go and proclaim the kingdom of God." What happened to this second "virtual disciple" Luke does not say.

The third would-be disciple said to Jesus, "I will follow you, Lord, but let me first say farewell to those at my home." Another reasonable request. To be nice Jesus could have said, "By all means, go and say good-bye, and pass along my greetings to your family." But instead Jesus says, "No one who puts a hand to the plow and looks back is fit for the kingdom of God" (9:62).

In the days before farm machinery (and in many parts of the world today), people plowed with only muscle power, that is, human and animal. A person guiding a plow had to look forward, focusing all strength on the plow to keep it going straight. Looking backward would cause the plow to go crooked, or even to pop out of the earth. Plowing while looking back would be about as effective as driving a car forward while looking backward over your shoulder. It just won't work. Those whose attention is elsewhere cannot follow Jesus. What happened to this third "virtual disciple" Luke does not say.

As Jesus encountered these three would-be disciples, he spoke to each the word that was most needed. Jesus was not interested in having disciples who imagined following him without ever leaving home. Jesus never promised that following him would be easy, safe, or "virtual."

Questions and Prayer

1. Why wasn't Jesus nicer to the three "virtual disciples"?

2. What do you think the three "virtual disciples" would have missed by staying home?

Prayer: Lord Jesus, you speak to each person the word that is most needed. Help me to hear your word today and to follow where you lead. Amen.

Saturday

Read Luke 11:14-22. *"When one stronger than he attacks him and overpowers him, he takes away his armor in which he trusted and divides his plunder"* (v. 22).

The Bible calls Jesus many things: Lamb, Son of God, Bridegroom, Savior, Word, to name a few. Unlike these noble names, *robber* does not seem to fit Jesus at all. Yet Jesus told a parable in which he gave himself the part of a robber who plunders a strongman's house. Jesus told this story to show that he was not an ally of Satan, as some of his detractors claimed, but an enemy of Satan (11:14-20). The parable of the robber sheds light on Jesus' conflict with death and evil, a conflict in which he triumphed once and for all by the cross and his resurrection.

"When a strong man, fully armed, guards his castle," said Jesus, "his property is safe" (11:21). In recent journalism, the term *strongman* politely refers to a dictator who "rules by force." A strongman is like Satan, binding people with fear and controlling them with threats and violence. Such a strongman never willingly lets go of power. It must be taken from him by someone yet more powerful—or by someone with a completely different kind of power.

Jesus is more powerful, and his strength is much different from Satan's. Jesus' strength is holiness, mercy, and love. With these he has broken into the strongman's house and plundered it. Sin and death are the "armor" in which Satan has trusted and with which he terrorizes captive people. Jesus dared to raid the strongman's house, set the captives free, and share with them the "plunder," or the booty, of the whole contest (11:22). These riches are forgiveness, joy in God's presence now and forever, patience in suffering, and zeal for the Gospel. Everything the strongman tried to lock away, Jesus freely gives.

An open door can be the first clue of a break-in. When a door that is supposed to be locked is left open, it may mean that a robber has broken in. That's how it was on Easter, when the women found that the stone had been rolled away from the tomb. The open door signaled that "someone more powerful" had plundered the house of death.

Some icons (in Orthodox Christian art, for example) portray Jesus breaking into Satan's stronghold and taking away his keys. Such art celebrates Jesus' victory over death. In Revelation 1:17-18, the risen Jesus says, "Do not be afraid. I am the first, and the last, and the living one. I was dead, and see, I am alive for ever and ever; and I have the keys of death and of Hades." Jesus took those keys when he plundered Satan's house. Keys are the power of access. The same set of keys can be used for evil or good, depending on who possesses them. Keys can lock people in or out. Satan tried to lock people *out* of forgiveness, life, and joy, and lock them *in* a prison of sin, death, and fear. Evil plays upon fears, jangling them like a cold bunch of keys to taunt the captives. So it is when great powers fall into the wrong hands.

Jesus plundered Satan's house and took away the keys, for Jesus was the rightful owner all along. Jesus has the full set of keys for every door in time and eternity. Those keys are now firmly in the hands of one who is trustworthy and true. With those keys Jesus unlocks the blessings of forgiveness, faith, hope, and love. He opens wide the door to eternal life. This divine "robber" has plundered the fortress of death and has taken the keys away from the enemy. In the words of the great hymn writer Charles Wesley, "His kingdom cannot fail. He rules o'er earth and heaven. The keys of death and hell are to our Jesus given. Lift up your heart, lift up your voice; rejoice, again I say, rejoice!" (*Lutheran Book of Worship*, no. 171).

QUESTIONS AND PRAYER

1. Does the picture of Jesus breaking into Satan's stronghold and taking away the keys appeal to you? Why or why not?

2. What might such a picture teach about the work of Christ?

Prayer: O Jesus, your kingdom cannot fail. You rule over earth and heaven. The keys of death and hell are given to you. We rejoice in your victory. Amen.

SUNDAY OF THE PASSION (PALM SUNDAY)

Read Luke 19:35-40. "Blessed is the king who comes in the name of the Lord" (v. 38).

THE YEAR IS 1863, and Union troops have lined the road leading to the beach in Charleston, South Carolina. They cheer and salute their comrades, the black soldiers of the Fifty-fourth Infantry Division of Massachusetts. Abraham Lincoln's Emancipation Proclamation has allowed these African American men to serve in the armed forces of the United States.

These well-disciplined and experienced soldiers are on their way to attack a Confederate fort. Like many other battles in the Civil War, this one means certain death. These soldiers know full well, as do the crowds by the side of the road, that no matter how bravely they fight, most of them will not survive. But a fife and drum strike up a military tune as the battle flags of the Union army snap and flutter in the sea breeze. This brief moment of glory shines with disciplined courage—the courage to die for their children's freedom.

This story of sacrifice, with its brief moment of glory, is like Palm Sunday when Jesus rode into Jerusalem. Shouting praises, the crowd spread cloaks along the road for Jesus to ride upon. Jesus knew that he advanced toward death on a cross. Jesus was the one-man army of God passing in review. He was both general and soldier, king and slave. He carried no gun or sword; his weapons were courage, obedience, and love. His uniform was humility; this was his glory.

Along the parade route the people were shouting, "Blessed is the king who comes in the name of the Lord! Peace in heaven, and glory in the highest heaven" (19:38). But some of the Pharisees in the crowd were annoyed by the cheering. To them, Jesus was no king or hero. "Teacher," they demanded, "order your disciples to stop." But Jesus answered, "I tell you, if these [people] were silent, the very stones would shout out" (v. 40).

Jesus had no chariot, or even a sturdy cavalry horse, only a humble beast of burden. Even this colt (or donkey) was borrowed (19:30-35). The colt on which Jesus rode is remembered as a fulfillment of prophecy (Isa. 62:11; Zech. 9:9) and a sign of humility (Matt. 21:5). But fulfillment and humility are not the same as timidity; soon after entering Jerusalem, Jesus drove the money changers from the temple with all the fury of soldiers liberating a captive fort.

With the temple reclaimed for God, Jesus went there every day to teach. The people loved to listen to him and were spellbound by his teaching. But this was only a lull before the great and final battle that now lay ahead, a conflict that meant certain death.

QUESTIONS AND PRAYER

1. What place do images of conflict and combat have in the Christian life (see Eph. 6:10-17)?

2. Why do you think the people in the temple were spellbound by Jesus' teaching?

Prayer: Lord Jesus, you entered Jerusalem to meet your death. You faced that great enemy so that we could have life in your name. Blessed are you, the king who comes in the name of the Lord. Amen.

Week 7: Dying and Rising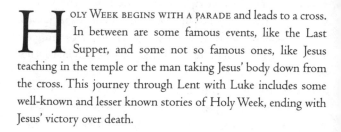

HOLY WEEK BEGINS WITH A PARADE and leads to a cross. In between are some famous events, like the Last Supper, and some not so famous ones, like Jesus teaching in the temple or the man taking Jesus' body down from the cross. This journey through Lent with Luke includes some well-known and lesser known stories of Holy Week, ending with Jesus' victory over death.

MONDAY IN HOLY WEEK

Read Luke 20:9-16. *"Then the owner of the vineyard said, 'What shall I do? I will send my beloved son; perhaps they will respect him'"* (v. 13).

EARLIER IN HIS MINISTRY, Jesus taught about forgiveness, prayer, and faith. Now, as he faced the cross, he taught about his own death and its significance for the world. In the temple he had so recently cleansed, Jesus told this story about what would soon happen to him.

Once there was a vineyard owner who leased his land to tenants and left the country. Time passed and the harvest came. The vineyard owner sent a servant to the tenants to collect his share of the produce. But the tenants beat the servant and sent him away empty-handed. The owner sent another servant. The tenants beat him also, insulted him, and sent him away empty-handed. This happened yet a third time. Finally the owner of the vineyard said, "What shall I do? I will send my beloved son; perhaps they will respect him" (20:13). Seeing the son coming, the tenants decided to kill him and take the entire estate for themselves. And they did. This murder was premeditated, calculated, and deliberate.

Jesus then asked, "What then will the owner of the vineyard do to them?" (20:15). Within Jesus' question is an even more pointed question: "If you were God, what would you do if people rejected and killed your son?" There is no comfortable answer, no easy out. Jesus said, "The owner will come and destroy those tenants and give the vineyard to others" (20:16).

This parable describes Jesus' own situation at the beginning of Holy Week. He himself was the son who would be cast out of the vineyard and killed by the tenants, the very people who were supposed to be accountable to God. When the wicked tenants kill the owner's son, everything changes. The owner takes the vineyard away from the wicked tenants and gives it to someone else. This points to the beginning of Christian community as the new people of God in Christ. Lest there be any doubt about his meaning, Jesus went on to say, "The stone which the builders rejected has become the cornerstone" (20:17). God was about to build something entirely new, with Jesus' death as the foundation stone.

Some have seized upon this story as a justification for persecuting Jewish people. But just as a mirror is intended to reflect one's own face, and not someone else's, so are Jesus' parables about us and not others. The parable's warning applies to all of us who find ourselves working in the vineyard, the church *now*. We will be held accountable for our own stewardship.

The story of the wicked tenants is a warning. The truth is, nobody wants to be a tenant. Rather than be accountable to God, human beings naturally prefer to be in charge, to own everything themselves. If God tries to hold people accountable, the solution is simple: Kill the messenger. Human pretense and rebellion later erupt in the cries of the crowd, "Crucify him, crucify him!" (23:21). Jesus' parable warns that those who put themselves in the place of God and reject the Son will be destroyed (20:16).

The story of the wicked tenants is also a promise. God loved the world so much that he sent his only son. God could destroy the vineyard, but instead God keeps searching for people who will believe and serve there faithfully. The vineyard is given to those who believe in and serve Jesus.

Questions and Prayer

1. How does the warning in Jesus' parable of the wicked tenants apply to you?

2. How does its promise apply to you?

Prayer: O God, human beings have so often rejected your prophets and despised your son. Have mercy on us. Give a day of grace, and give us another chance to serve. Amen.

Tuesday in Holy Week

Read Luke 21:25-28. *"When these things begin to take place, stand up and raise your heads, because your redemption is drawing near" (v. 28).*

THUNDER RUMBLES UNDER GRAY CLOUDS as lightning licks the horizon. An eerie stillness pervades the air. Even the birds have stopped singing. Children are called inside, windows are closed, radios are tuned to the weather station. The sky turns grayish green as tornado sirens pierce the air. Plans for that day are quickly abandoned. Daily routines are scrapped. All that matters is living through the storm.

A great storm was brewing in Jerusalem during Holy Week, with Jesus at the center of it. With his own betrayal and cross just days away, Jesus does not take cover from the storm. Jesus does nothing to save himself. It would have been easy for him to slip out of town, hide out, and save his own life. But instead Jesus stayed in public view. He even had a daily routine. Every day Jesus taught in the temple, and then he would go and spend each night on the Mount of Olives just outside of town. He returned to Jerusalem each morning and "all the people would get up early in the morning to listen to him in the Temple" (21:38).

Jesus followed this regimen during the first days of Holy Week, yet his teaching was anything but routine. As he faced his own death, he spoke about suffering and persecution, and the world coming to an end. He even said that the Son of Man will come "in a cloud with power and great glory" (21:27). Jesus' teachings during Holy Week are about as comforting as a tornado siren. Just as the purpose of a siren is to save life, so Jesus' purpose is to save. "People will faint from fear and foreboding of what is coming upon the world, for the powers of the heavens will be shaken," Jesus said (v. 26). God's people must keep alert and be ready to "stand before the Son of Man" (v. 36).

Luke's Gospel begins and ends with the hope of redemption. Like labor pains that lead to delivery and then birth, Jesus' teachings during Holy Week bring hope for the world's redemption. *Redemption* means "restoring something to a rightful place": like when a wedding ring lying neglected in a pawnshop is bought back, restored to its rightful owner; or a hostage is rescued and restored to his loving family; or a people once enslaved are restored to freedom. It may take a crisis, a conflict, or a storm to bring about such redemption. Jesus prepares for the storm not by taking shelter from it but by living and dying in the eye of the storm and remaining ever obedient to God.

Near the beginning of Luke's Gospel, Anna the prophet told all who awaited the redemption of Israel to look to Jesus (2:38). Now, at the end of the Gospel, Jesus promises that "the Son of Man" will come "in a cloud with power and great glory." "When these things begin to take place," Jesus said, "stand up and raise your heads, because your redemption is drawing near" (21:28).

Look to Jesus for redemption! He is coming soon! Some Christians claim to know when Jesus will return, as though they can decipher world events in light of verses such as Luke 21:24. Instead of looking to Jesus for redemption, perhaps the authors of best-selling prophecy books are looking to their publishers for royalties. But other Christians have a different problem—the problem of not paying attention to Jesus' teachings at all, as though God has given people an infinite line of credit with no day of reckoning.

Neither of these options—predicting the future or ignoring Jesus' teachings—is a good way to watch for redemption. During Holy Week and every week, it is better to walk with Jesus to the cross, and wait there for Easter.

Questions and Prayer

1. Where in the Christian life do Jesus' teachings about the end of the world have a place? For example, are these teachings at the center of faith or on the edges?

2. What does it mean to you to "wait for redemption"?

Prayer: Lord God, the whole Christian church confesses this about Jesus: "I believe that he will come again to judge the living and the dead, and his kingdom shall have no end." Bless the church with expectation as we await his coming. Amen.

Wednesday in Holy Week

Luke 22:3-6. *"Then Satan entered into Judas called Iscariot, who was one of the twelve"* (v. 3).

JESUS GATHERED SUCH A FOLLOWING in the temple that his enemies dared not arrest him there or anywhere in public, lest they touch off a riot. His arrest would have to be done secretly. Only someone close to Jesus could name the right time and place. One day Jesus' enemies received a visit from one of the disciples, offering information on where and when Jesus could be arrested. This disciple would be paid for his services.

Until now, Judas has barely figured into the Gospel story. Given what little Luke tells us, Judas seems to have been a very ordinary person. Other disciples and followers, such as Mary, Martha, or Joseph of Arimathea, have their moments in the spotlight, but Judas is hardly noticed until he betrays Jesus. A list of other disciples whom Jesus called ends with a reference to Judas, who "became a betrayer" (6:16).

Because he was a traitor, Judas is sometimes seen as a villain larger than life. Yet he may have been just a disgruntled disciple with a petty grievance, a malcontent who simply wanted some return for all his months of following Jesus. Satan "entered into" Judas (22:3) and used him for evil. God, in turn, brought good out of this great evil by raising Jesus from the dead. But Judas himself appears to have been unremarkable.

The world has seen villains come and go, and some have dealt in death on a grand scale. Adolf Hitler's name has come to stand for all that's evil. Josef Stalin, between puffs on his cigarette and with no show of remorse, could sign a death warrant for thousands of innocent people. Millions died in front of his firing squads or starved to death in isolated labor camps on the tundra above the Arctic Circle. In return for this evil, Stalin controlled the largest empire in the world.

Judas, in contrast, simply gave some information, for which he received a small sum of money—thirty pieces of silver, according to Matthew 26:15, the standard price for a slave. It was enough money for Judas to live on for a while, a kind of severance pay after he quit the job of following Jesus. It all sounds very ordinary, very mundane, compared with the grand scale of evil such as that which occurred in the twentieth century.

And yet, what could be worse than helping to arrange for the murder of the Son of God? Jesus himself said, "Woe to that one by whom the Son of Man is betrayed!" (22:22). It is Judas' very ordinariness that is most frightening, for each person, even each follower of Jesus, is capable of betraying the Master. Ordinary feelings like resentment and envy, even everyday sins like unbelief or anger, can lead to larger betrayals. Part of the Lenten journey is to see ourselves in the place of the disciples, including the place of Judas.

Of course, it is easier it is to identify with Peter than with Judas. Peter is lovable despite all his flaws, or maybe because of them. One can admire Peter's bold confession that Jesus is the Christ, identify with Peter's agony after he has denied Jesus three times, thrill with Peter when he runs to the empty tomb on Easter. Jesus loves Peter, forgives him, and challenges him to grow beyond even his worst failings: "I have prayed for you that your own faith may not fail," Jesus says to Peter, "and . . . once you have turned back, strengthen your brothers" (22:32). There is great comfort in Jesus' love for Peter.

But it is otherwise with Judas. Judas sat with Jesus at the Last Supper, that most sacred and intimate meal, feigning love and loyalty. That night, Judas helped Jesus' enemies to arrest him in the Garden of Gethsemane, where he had gone with his disciples to pray. It was all so easy to arrange. Judas led the crowd of soldiers and priests by night. And lest the officers in the darkness arrest the wrong man, Judas even identified Jesus with a kiss.

The story of Judas, the ordinary person into whom Satan entered, is a disturbing reminder of the power of sin, even among the followers of Jesus. When at the Last Supper the disciples ask one another which of them could possibly betray Jesus, Jesus does not tell them. Each one must live with the question, "Lord, is it I?"

QUESTIONS AND PRAYER

1. What comes to mind when you think of Judas?

2. Could any one of the disciples have betrayed Jesus?

3. If so, what does this suggest about the Christian life?

Prayer: Holy Spirit, guard us against the temptations to betray Jesus in our thoughts, words, and deeds. Keep us steadfast in faith, as Christ is faithful to us. Amen.

THURSDAY IN HOLY WEEK

Read Luke 22:39-46. *"Pray that you may not come into the time of trial"* (v. 40).

IN JERUSALEM, IN A LARGE UPPER ROOM, Jesus ate the Passover meal of bread and wine with his disciples. He told them, "I have eagerly desired to eat this Passover with you before I suffer; I tell you, I will not eat it again until it is fulfilled in the kingdom of God" (22:16). Though Jesus had celebrated many a Passover before, this night was different from all others. At other Passover meals, the people recalled how God had saved Israel from slavery in Egypt and made them a covenant people. But when Jesus ate the Passover with his disciples, he made a new covenant sealed with his own body and blood. Jesus was preparing to give his own life to lead people out of the bondage of sin and death into new, eternal life with God.

When the meal was finished, Jesus and his disciples walked from Jerusalem to the Mount of Olives. The steep path led down into a rocky valley. Olive trees dotted the slopes where a few ancient tombs were set along the hillside. Soon they came to the Garden of Gethsemane. It was a peaceful place, secluded yet close enough to the city that the disciples could see lamplight flickering in the windows of Jerusalem.

Although it was Jesus' custom to pray here on the Mount of Olives, this night would be different. He told the disciples, "Pray that you may not enter into temptation" (22:40). Early on, Jesus had taught the disciples to pray, "Lead us not into temptation" (11:4b). That request was often just one among others in the Lord's Prayer, but tonight this particular plea was more intense, more vivid, more urgent than any other prayer.

Temptations were rising around Jesus and his disciples like a flood. The disciples would either resist or be swept away, leaving all their good intentions of courage, loyalty, and obedience far behind. No matter how much Jesus wanted his disciples to stand faithfully with him, he must have known that he would have to stand trial and meet death alone.

"Pray that you may not enter into temptation," Jesus told the disciples. Then he withdrew from them to pray by himself. "Father, if you are willing, take this cup from me. Nevertheless, not my will but yours be done" (22:42). There in the Garden of Gethsemane, Jesus strove to submit completely to the Father's will. Only God knows what anguish Jesus endured as Jesus prayed with "loud cries and tears" to God who was able to save him from death. (Heb. 5:7). Jesus' constant prayer against temptation was "not my will but yours be done." As Jesus continued in the spirit of this prayer throughout his trial and crucifixion, he was tempted in every way that we are, but without sin (Heb. 4:15).

"Father, if you are willing, take this cup from me," Jesus prayed. No one can force another person to drink; the bitter cup of suffering must be accepted willingly or not at all. There in the Garden of Gethsemane, Jesus could have chosen to slip away into the night. He could have escaped the cross. But instead Jesus wrestled in prayer, conforming his will to God's. Jesus' struggle for perfect obedience was so intense that, according to some ancient texts, his sweat became like great drops of blood, falling on the ground as he prayed (22:44).

At last, Jesus rose from prayer and came to the disciples. It would have comforted him to find them all praying. But "because of grief," they were sleeping (22:45). Jesus woke them: "Get up and pray that you may not come into the time of trial" (22:46). As he was speaking, Judas led a crowd of soldiers to this place of prayer. Judas approached Jesus to betray him with a kiss.

QUESTIONS AND PRAYER

1. When has the prayer "lead us not into temptation" been most urgent for you?

2. What do you think Luke meant by saying that the disciples were sleeping "because of grief"?

Prayer: O Jesus, before the soldiers came to Gethsemane, you could have vanished into the night and escaped the cross. But instead you stayed to do God's will. For this we thank and praise you. Amen.

FRIDAY IN HOLY WEEK

Read Luke 23:33, 39-43. *"They crucified Jesus there with the criminals, one on his right and one on his left"* (v. 33).

THIS PRAYER FOR GOOD FRIDAY is based on Luke 23:39-43 and uses the T.R.I.P.© devotional pattern of Thanksgiving, Regret, Intercession, and Purpose.

Thanksgiving: Lord Jesus, what you suffered on the cross is beyond our ability to imagine. From the cross, you poured out God's love for the world. On the cross, you bore all human sin and death. You became a prisoner so that we could be set free. You were abandoned so that we could be adopted. You were despised so that we could be loved. You died so that we might live.

By your side, a dying criminal said, "Jesus, remember me when you come into your kingdom" (23:42). And you promised, "Truly, I say to you, today you will be with me in paradise" (v. 43). Thank you for your mercy and loving kindness to everyone who turns to you and calls your name. We bless you for your mercy, we praise you for your love.

Regret: The other criminal who was crucified beside you said, "Are you not the Messiah? Save yourself and us!" (23:39). We have said or thought this too, and we confess and repent that it is so easy to despise your cross. You don't look like you are in charge when you are hanging there. When we see the cross, it is hard to believe that you are God with us. We expected something else from God, not this. When we or our loved ones suffer, when we see people in pain, we could shout, "Aren't you the Messiah? Save yourself and us!" But rather than stop all the suffering, you took it upon yourself and into yourself. We regret having despised your cross. We repent of this unbelief and ask you to forgive us.

Intercession: Lord Jesus, one of the criminals who died with you received your promise to enter paradise with you. We pray, Lord, for people who have committed crimes. Transform these brothers and sisters by the power of the Holy Spirit. Lead them to repentance and faith in you. Help them to amend their lives with you and with other people. Bless and strengthen chaplains and those who work in prison ministries.

You were falsely accused and punished for crimes you did not commit. In your name we remember prisoners who are falsely accused. May they endure in hope that the truth will come to light, and may they be set free from unjust punishment. Help us to work for greater justice so that innocent people will not go to jail. We pray also for those who suffer because they follow you, Lord Jesus. Sustain these disciples with your presence, and show us how to support and encourage them. Lord Jesus, great crimes were committed against you. We intercede for all those against whom wrong has been done, that they may share your victory over evil.

Purpose: Lord Jesus, today we look at your cross and see you there with two criminals. One criminal despised your cross, the other received your promise. You call us to believe that your cross gives life, to trust that with you all things are possible and that no human being is beyond your reach. Your suffering and your love move us to pray not only for ourselves but for our brothers and sisters: "Jesus, remember us, when you come into your kingdom."

QUESTION AND PRAYER

I. Why do you think Jesus was crucified between two criminals?

Prayer: Use the T.R.I.P.© devotion above as today's prayer.

SATURDAY IN HOLY WEEK

Read Luke 23:50-56. *Now there was a good and righteous man named Joseph, . . . and he was waiting expectantly for the kingdom of God* (vv. 50, 51).

THE FUNERAL AT THE COUNTRY CHURCH WAS OVER, and the procession of cars began to follow the hearse to the cemetery. A visitor from the city, riding with the deceased's relatives, was surprised to see cars that were not in the funeral procession pulling over to the side of the road. After asking why these cars pulled over, the visitor was told, "It's a sign of respect that we show for the person who has died and their family. Everyone stops for a funeral."

Imagine, a sign of respect at the time of death! Jesus' death had been anything but respectable. He was mocked, abused, and abandoned to die with criminals. The people who loved Jesus could only watch and wait. After Jesus was dead, these faithful few found ways to show their respect and love. The story of the women who brought spices to the tomb is well known, but another person who paid his respects is often overlooked.

That person was Joseph of Arimathea, a good and righteous man who had disagreed with the plan to put Jesus to death. Joseph was a prominent man, described by Luke as "a member of the council"(23:50). Pilate released the body of Jesus to Joseph for burial. To go to Pilate and ask for Jesus' body was risky. Coming out as a supporter of Jesus—even after his death—might provoke Jesus' enemies. Nevertheless, Joseph got Pilate's consent and took the broken body down from the cross. The next step was to give the body a decent burial. So Joseph wrapped the body of Jesus in a linen shroud and "laid it in a rock-hewn tomb where no one had ever been laid" (v. 53). The tomb may have been purchased by Joseph for himself and his family and was probably very expensive. This was the way in which Joseph paid his respects.

At last, Joseph had to entrust Jesus into the care of God. Having placed the body of Jesus in the tomb, there was nothing more to do but walk away. Luke does not describe this moment, but most people know how hard it can be to walk away from the grave of a loved one, leaving the past, present, and future completely in God's care. This, too, is part of waiting expectantly for the kingdom of God, giving up claims on the deceased and letting God be God.

The Saturday between Good Friday and Easter is a strange time, a time of "waiting expectantly for the kingdom of God" (23:51). As the day after Good Friday, it is a day to pay our respects to Jesus by remembering his death. Like the drivers on that country road pulling aside to honor the funeral procession, Christians around the world pause to ponder what God has done. It is a day to look back at what happened on the cross and to pay our respects. It is a day to "rest" (23:56), because Jesus has finished his work.

But this day is also the Saturday before Easter—a day to prepare for a great celebration, a day to expect resurrection. It is a day to anticipate Jesus' triumph over death and to receive his promise of resurrection for all who believe in him. This is a day for expecting the kingdom of God. To those who wait, the time between death and resurrection is very long. For God, it is but a moment.

Questions and Prayer

1. To whom and in what ways do we pay our respects when someone has died?

2. In terms of devotion or religious observance, what do you usually do on the Saturday before Easter?

Prayer: O Lord, after you died, your body was taken down from the cross and laid to rest in a new tomb. With you are laid to rest our sins and fears, even the fear of death. With you we watch for morning. Amen.

Easter Sunday

Read Luke 24:1-12. *"They found the stone rolled away from the tomb"* (v. 2).

THE DAY AFTER A BIG STOCK MARKET CRASH, investors big and small crawled out from under the wreckage to survey the damages. Although financial superheroes had lost billions of dollars, the real story was how much ordinary folks had lost. No one knew how long it would take the market to recover. Some financial advisors said that after the crash was the best time to invest, to get stock at bargain prices. But for most investors, only a miracle would convince them to reinvest, that is, if they had anything left to invest.

The day after the crash—maybe that's what it was like for Jesus' followers after Good Friday. The disciples had ventured a lot for Jesus, leaving behind their work, home, and family. Following Jesus had looked so promising! He could heal the sick, cast out demons, speak with authority, and even forgive sins—something, it was thought, only God could do. The disciples hoped that with Jesus they had gotten in on the ground floor of the kingdom and could ride with Jesus all the way to the top. On Palm Sunday, when Jesus rode into Jerusalem and the crowds cheered, "Hosanna!" the disciples' stock in Jesus soared. At the Last Supper, they argued about who would have the best place in the kingdom.

Then came the Good Friday crash. When Jesus died on the cross, the disciples lost everything. All their hopes were crucified with the Master. Joseph gave Jesus' body a decent burial, and the disciples buried their hearts with him. On the first day of the week a few close friends of Jesus got up very early. As people today take flowers to the grave of a loved one, these women took burial spices to Jesus' tomb. As they walked silently to the tomb, they knew that they'd lost a fortune in love. Nothing remained but their desire to bring burial spices to the tomb.

As the women approached Jesus' tomb, the cover of night began to lift. Something about the tomb looked strange. In the morning mist, the burial cave should have been all gray. But in the half light, the women spied a black opening in the rock. The entrance to the tomb was open. The stone was rolled away. Silently the women entered the tomb. In the dim light they expected to see a human form shrouded in white, lying on a stone ledge. But there was no shrouded form. The ledge at the wall of the cave was bare. The tomb was empty.

The women were perplexed and confused, when suddenly two men in dazzling clothes stood beside them. The women bowed low, shielding their eyes from the light. "Why do you seek the living among the dead?" the messengers asked (24:5). What a strange question. The women were not seeking the living among the dead; they were seeking the dead. The messengers continued, "He is not here, but has risen. Remember how he told you, while he was still in Galilee, that the Son of Man must be handed over to sinners, and be crucified, and on the third day rise again" (24:5-7). Now the truth dawned on the women. Jesus had risen. The Master, the Friend, the Teacher, the Savior, the Son, lives.

The disciples invested everything in Jesus and lost, or so it seemed. The truth is, Jesus invested everything in them—in us— and won. The crash on Good Friday shook the world. But that crash was the sound of Satan's kingdom falling, like a big jailhouse opened by an earthquake. Jesus broke it down with obedience and love. Then he broke death's grip by walking out of the tomb. "Jesus is not here. He is risen!"

QUESTIONS AND PRAYER

1. In what ways do people "seek the living among the dead"?
2. What is the message of Easter, according to Luke 24:7?

Prayer: O Jesus, you burst the bonds of death and rose victorious from the grave. Because of you, we have new life now and forever. We praise and bless your holy name. Amen.

WORKS CITED

Hugo, Victor. *Les Misérables* (1862), Book I, chapter 6; Book II, chapters 3, 5–6, 12. May 1994 <wiretap.area.com/Gopher/Library/Classic/lesmis.vh>.

King, Martin Luther. From *The Speeches of Martin Luther King, Jr.* (Orland Park, Ill.: MPI Media Group, 1988).

Luther, Martin. The Large Catechism. In *The Book of Concord: The Confessions of the Evangelical Lutheran Church,* trans. and ed., Theodore Tappert, et al. (Philadelphia: Fortress Press, 1959), 433.

———. "Introduction to the Lord's Prayer." *The Small Catechism* (Minneapolis: Augsburg Fortress, 1979), 17.

Mount Carmel Ministries. *Daily Texts 2000* (Alexandria, Minn.: Mount Carmel Ministries, 2000).

New York Times News Service. "Russian Prince Becomes Squatter to Gain Ancestral Land." *Dallas Morning News* (8 January 2000).

Niebuhr, H. Richard. *The Kingdom of God in America* (New York: Harper and Row, 1937), 193.

Thomas, Gary. "The Forgiveness Factor." *Christianity Today* (10 January 2000): 38–45.

The Voice of the Martyrs. *Persecution.com: A Global Perspec:'ve on Persecution of God's Children.* Feb. 2000 <www.persecution.com>.

Wesley, Charles. "Rejoice, the Lord Is King!" no. 171. Tune by William E. Fischer. *Lutheran Book of Worship* (Minneapolis: Augsburg Publishing House, 1978).

ACKNOWLEDGMENTS

THE AUTHOR THANKS Craig Koester for his thoughts on Judas (Luke 22:3-6) and for descriptions of specific biblical places. The devotion on Luke 12:8-12 (the "unforgivable sin") retells and reflects on an encounter that Craig and I had while walking home from church one day in New York City. Thanks also to Johan Hinderlie and Mt. Carmel Ministries for the T.R.I.P.© guide to prayer and Bible study.